BOOTLEG

KAREN BLUMENTHAL

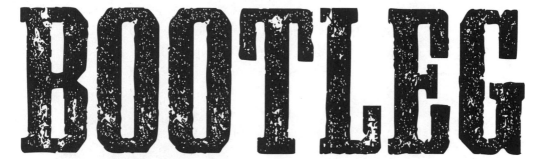

BOOTLEG

MURDER, MOONSHINE, AND
THE LAWLESS YEARS OF PROHIBITION

Flash
Point

ROARING BROOK PRESS

NEW YORK

Frontispiece: A young boy on the islands of St. Pierre and Miquelon perches on liquor crates that were emptied so their contents could be smuggled to the United States.

Text copyright © 2011 by Karen Blumenthal

Published by Flash Point, an imprint of Roaring Brook Press

Roaring Brook Press is a division of Holtzbrinck Publishing Holdings Limited Partnership

175 Fifth Avenue, New York, New York 10010

macteenbooks.com

Library of Congress Cataloging-in-Publication Data

Blumenthal, Karen.

Bootleg : murder, moonshine, and the lawless years of prohibition / Karen Blumenthal.—1st ed.

p. cm.

ISBN 978-1-59643-449-3

1. Prohibition—United States—Juvenile literature. 2. Temperance—United States—History—20th century—Juvenile literature. 3. Alchoholic beverage industry—United States—History—20th century—Juvenile literature. 4. Alchoholic beverage law violations— United States—History—20th century—Juvenile literature. 5. United States—History—1919–1933—Juvenile literature. I. Title.

HV5089.B66 2011

363.4'1097309042—dc22

2010032687

Roaring Brook Press books are available for special promotions and premiums. For details contact: Director of Special Markets, Holtzbrinck Publishers.

First edition 2011

Book design by Jay Colvin

Printed in the United States of America

3   5   7   9   8   6   4

CONTENTS

VALENTINE'S DAY 1929

SOMETIME AFTER 10 A.M. on this shivery-cold and windy Chicago morning, seven men gathered in a nondescript garage warehouse on Clark Street.

Most of them were wearing hats and coats against the chill of the nearly empty warehouse as they waited, maybe for a big shipment of smuggled whiskey, maybe for a special meeting. These were no Boy Scouts. All had ties to a criminal gang run by George "Bugs" Moran, a slow-moving, slow-thinking thug who was supposed to be on his way to the garage. Most of them had done some jail time. One, a mechanic, maintained the gang's trucks, which delivered illegal beer and liquor to Chicago bars and nightclubs, a thriving business despite laws that banned the sale of alcoholic beverages. Another owned an illegal nightclub. A third was the business manager for Moran. There was an optometrist, who just liked hanging out with the gangsters, and three muscle men, who often carried out the gang's dirty work.

On the snow-dusted street outside, a black Cadillac with a police gong, siren, and gun rack—the type usually driven by police detectives—pulled up to the

A crowd gathers outside the Clark Street garage as officials remove the victims of the St. Valentine's Day murders.

Investigators take a look at bullet holes left behind by a machine gun in a Chicago gangland shooting in the mid-1920s.

curb. Four or five men emerged, two dressed like police officers, and went into the warehouse. Seeing the "officers" and apparently thinking local cops were conducting a routine alcohol raid, the seven men inside lined up against the back wall and put their hands in the air.

They were still in that vulnerable position when two machine guns started firing.

CHICAGO POLICE had seen dozens of gangland murders as rival gangs fought over who could provide bootleg beer and liquor to the city's many neighborhoods. But they had never seen anything as gruesome as this massacre of seven men.

It wasn't supposed to be this way. Starting nearly a century before, small groups of religious and morally minded citizens had tried to solve a growing problem of drunkenness by encouraging moderation in drinking and then, later, abstinence from alcohol. The crusade had gradually gained steam and in 1920, the Eighteenth Amendment to the U.S. Constitution had outlawed the manufacture, sale, and transportation of liquor. Prohibition, as it was called, was a grand social revolution that was supposed to forever end drunkenness, reduce crime, and make life better for America's families.

Nine years later, the results were quite different. People who had always followed the rules now openly ignored the highest law of the land. Children helped their parents secretly concoct brews. Young people carried flasks of whiskey in their pockets to look fashionable and hung out at illegal "speakeasies," drinking. Teenage boys acted as lookouts for bootleggers or drove cars and boats loaded with illegal liquor to big cities.

As alcohol was sold all around them, police officers, public officials, judges, and politicians took bribes or looked the other way. Gangsters like Bugs Moran and the notorious Al Capone divided and controlled some of the nation's biggest cities, and now they seemed to murder each other at will. Rather than become more moral and upright, America, in the eyes of many, had become a lawless society.

How had such good intentions gone so terribly, terribly wrong?

CHAPTER 1
THE LITTLE SHEPPARD

Looking back on the childhood of Morris Sheppard, you can see glimmers of a budding statesman, the kind of earnest political leader who would want to make a big difference in the world.

Born in 1875, little Morris learned poetry and literary passages before he was old enough to recognize his ABCs. As a toddler, he would stand on the counter of a local store in rural East Texas and recite verses for a stick of candy, continuing until his pockets couldn't hold another piece.

Attending schools in small Texas towns like Daingerfield, Black Jack, and Pittsburg, he studied Greek, Latin, history, and English and developed persuasive skills and an apparent flair for leadership. At 13, he shared with some other boys the story of William Tell, the legendary marksman who shot an apple off his son's head with a bow and arrow. Admiring Tell's skill and bravery, but lacking the arrows, Morris and his friends decided to reenact the deed—with a gun.

"We are told," reported the *Pittsburg Press* in 1888, "that several boys stood with apples on their heads

Morris Sheppard rose from a child orator to become a powerful voice against liquor.

and Morris with a target rifle shot them off—that is to say, the apples, fortunately not their heads."

The boys' parents were horrified when they heard about the game and put a quick end to it. Morris escaped a whipping but got a stern lecture from his father, a local judge.

When Morris finished his regular schooling at 16, he moved on to the University of Texas in Austin. Jumping into student life at the young and still-small school, he joined a fraternity, led a literary society, played the cornet and piano, and sang in the glee club. Always fond of a good joke, he got a kick out of entering the dining hall by walking on his hands. But he was best known for his preacherlike speaking skills and was selected to compete in contests and serve as a graduation speaker.

From there he went to law school, spending two years in Austin and a third at Yale University in Connecticut. Once again, he attracted attention as a star orator, winning a debating prize and speaking at the graduation ceremonies.

Somewhere between his general-store recitations and his law degree, young Morris came to a heartfelt belief: He despised liquor and the saloons that sold it. He sometimes said his feelings grew out of his grammar school science classes, where he saw vivid drawings of a drunkard's stomach and read about how alcohol destroyed the human body.

He may have been influenced by the anti-liquor stance of the Methodist church, which he joined as a college student. His time at Yale also may have hardened his stance. He arrived there in debt and driven to succeed. So, he said, "I cut out every item of expense that was possible and quit every practice which might be injurious"—including tobacco, coffee, and tea. The result, he said, was "so satisfactory" that those items "remained on the contraband list ever since."

After Yale, young Morris began practicing law in East Texas, but in 1902, his career took an unexpected turn. His father, John, who had been elected to a second term in the U.S. House of Representatives, fell ill and then passed away. Friends immediately urged Morris to run for his father's seat.

Jumping in just ten days before the primary election, Morris stumped the

By the mid-1920s, when he posed with two youngsters in front of the Capitol, Sheppard was a senior statesman in Congress.

district, delivering an average of seven speeches a day. When his opponents made fun of his youth, he replied that it was something he "was overcoming day by day."

To nearly everyone's surprise, he won the seat. At the age of twenty-seven, he headed to Washington.

Small in stature at 5 feet, 7 inches, slight at 135 pounds, and youthful looking, Sheppard hardly looked like a Congressman. "It will take the older members

While most known for his glittery speeches, Sheppard (center, seated) also chaired a U.S. House Public Buildings and Grounds Committee in 1912.

some time to get to know Mr. Sheppard, so that they will not try to send him on errands," the *Washington Post* noted.

Nicknamed the "boy orator of Texas," Sheppard was originally known more for his speaking skills than for any special legislation. As the "boy" matured into a confident congressman, the world outside of Washington was changing. Debates that had simmered for years over whether alcohol was dangerous and should be legally banned were beginning to roll to a boil. Originally, the arguments took place community by community and county by county. But as the number of towns outlawing liquor sales and saloons multiplied, the organizers raised the ante, taking aim at entire states. To support their efforts, Sheppard introduced legislation to keep liquor from moving from wet areas—where liquor was legal— into dry ones, where liquor was outlawed.

In 1911, he actively campaigned to prohibit the sale of alcohol throughout Texas, openly supporting prohibition for the first time. Despite his efforts, the prohibition proposal fell a few thousand votes short in the hotly contested election.

In 1913, one of Texas's U.S. senators resigned. Sheppard outmaneuvered a more popular candidate, and the Texas legislature selected him to fill the powerful job as senator. In a colorful speech to the state legislature, he accepted his new job, calling for limits on working hours, clearer and simpler laws, and, with fiery eloquence, an end to liquor sales.

"The liquor traffic is a peril to society," he said. "I shall oppose this scourge from hell until my arm can strike no longer and my tongue can speak no more.

"I shall oppose it because I hear the cries of children who are hungering for bread. I shall oppose it because I see a mother's wasted face, her pale lips pleading with the besotted figure at her side.

"I shall oppose it because I see the staggering forms of men whose trembling hands hold but the ashes of their strength and pride.

He concluded, "I shall oppose it because its abolition will mean a new stability for the Republic, a new radiance for the flag."

Just months later, toward the end of 1913, the two biggest anti-liquor groups in the nation decided the time was right for an even more dramatic move. To end the scourge of alcohol now and for future generations, they proposed a national solution—not just a law, but an amendment to the U.S. Constitution that would forever ban the sale of liquor throughout the country. To champion their cause in the U.S. Senate, they turned to Morris Sheppard.

On a chilly winter day in December 1913, some 4,000 people gathered in Washington, D.C., to take crucial steps toward changing America's drinking habits once and for all. Leading the march were children.

At the very front, a young boy carried an American flag. Just behind him, dozens of girls in white dresses carried banners calling for a national prohibition on alcohol. Following them were Woman's Christian Temperance Union members from every state, many wearing the white ribbons that symbolized prohibition. Some sang their anthem, "A Saloonless Nation by 1920."

Sheppard was elected to the Senate in 1913.

Joining from another direction were the men of the Anti-Saloon League. Together, they marched to the Capitol. Waiting on the steps to receive a proposed constitutional amendment were Senator Sheppard and Representative Richmond Pearson Hobson of Alabama.

Later that day, Sheppard introduced this constitutional amendment in Congress for the first time, saying, "The fact that alcohol undermines the brain and paralyzes the will of man, planting in him and his posterity the seeds of physical and moral degeneracy, the seeds of disease, the seeds of poverty, the seeds of crime, makes it a peril to the very existence of free government. Let the people of this Nation insert in the National Constitution, the source of the Nation's life, a clause prohibiting an evil that will prove to be the source of the nation's death."

Results might take years. But with patience and determination, Sheppard and his supporters could—and would—change the culture, the behavior, and the course of America.

For his role, Morris Sheppard would be known as the Father of National Prohibition. It would turn out to be a most dubious distinction.

Woman's Christian Temperance Union and Anti-Saloon League members march toward the Capitol in 1913 to present a proposed prohibition amendment to the U.S. Constitution.

THE GREAT REVIVAL

of

TEN NIGHTS IN A BAR ROOM

IS THE GRANDEST DRAMATIC EVENT IN THE HISTORY OF THE 19TH CENTURY

A PLAY WHICH HAS EVERYWHERE PROVEN A SENSATION UNPARALLELED IN THE HISTORY OF THE DRAMA.

THE SOBS AND TEARS OF SYMPATHY

From auditors of all sexes and ages, who come to witness this truthful picture, are evidences of its wonderful dramatic power. Over 100,000 persons, heads of families, members of churches, all interested in the propagation of the great principles of temperance, have born testimony to the

LIFE-LIKE DELINEATORS OF FOLLY, MISERY MADNESS AND CRIME

CAUSED BY THE BRUTAL, DISGUSTING AND DEMORALIZING VICE OF DRUNKENNESS.

This beautiful drama depicts a series of truthful scenes in the course of a drunkard's life. Some of them are touching in the extreme, some are dark and terrible. Step by step is portrayed the downward course of the tempting vender and his infatuated victim until both involved in hopeless ruin. The play is marred by no exaggerations, but exhibits the actualities of life with a severe simplicity and adherence with that gives to every picture a photographic vividness. The large audiences seem to be in full sympathy with the moral of the story, laugh at Sample Switchel, sympathize with poor drunken Joe Morgan, and weep at

THE DEATH OF LITTLE MARY

AN ENTERTAINMENT FOR EVERYBODY.   INTERESTING TO ALL

REMOVING THE BARRIER BETWEEN PULPIT AND STAGE.

NEW MUSIC! SONGS! DANCES!

SEE THE BEST RENDITION OF THE PLAY YOU EVER SAW. YOU WILL

OF MIRTH, PATHOS, COMEDY AND SENSATION.

"Father, deaf father, come home with me now"

ENDORSED BY THE PRESS, CLERGY AND CRITICS OF ALL CREEDS AND DENOMINATIONS

YOU WILL SEE A FIRST-CLASS COMPANY OF LADIES AND GENTLEMEN. A FIRST-CLASS PERFORMANCE.   MAGNIFICENT SCENERY.   NEW STAGE SETTINGS

A FEW REASONS WHY

YOU SEE TEN NIGHTS IN A BAR ROOM

CHAPTER 2
HOT AND COLD WATER

DRINKING and debates about it date back almost to the founding of America. Long before Morris Sheppard, arguments about alcohol had prompted the first rebellion in the new country, fueled some of the nation's first social movements, and helped launch women into politics, preparing them for their fight for the right to vote.

The Pilgrims brought beer and hard liquors with them on the *Mayflower*. Later the Puritans learned to distill rum. The earliest settlers were fond of "strong waters" and "hot waters." Those "waters" may have been safer than regular creek or well water, but also had considerably more mind-fuzzing alcohol than beer or fermented fruit-based drinks like wine and cider.

By the mid-1700s, the new land was awash in various kinds of alcoholic beverages. Rum was almost a form of money, paid as wages and exchanged for basic goods. Gin was cheaper and probably more powerful, given its nicknames "Strip and Go Naked" and "Blue Ruin." Apple cider was widely available in a distilled, or "hard," version known as

A playbill highlights the sobering message of Ten Nights in a Bar Room, *a popular, long-running temperance play.*

applejack or Jersey Lightning. Using fermentation processes first discovered by ancient civilizations thousands of years ago, pears became "perry" in New England, honey became mead in Vermont, and Georgia peaches made a fine brandy.

Residents came to expect a good drink almost everywhere—at holiday celebrations and funerals, in taverns, at community meetings, and at polling places. In 1758, a politician from Virginia named George Washington, who was running for the House of Burgesses, bought brandy, rum, cider, beer, and wine for those who turned up to vote, spending a total of thirty-seven pounds, seven shillings. He won.

Hard liquor was so important to both health and morale that members of the Continental Army got a daily ration. As its leader, General Washington enjoyed a

wide range of choices, drinking champagne, cider, brandy, beer, rum, and wine. During his first three months as president, hard liquor was one of his largest expenses, though he was a moderate drinker himself. Later he would operate a major whiskey distillery at Mount Vernon.

By the late eighteenth century, the new Americans were serious drinkers, with those over age fifteen each consuming, on average, more than five gallons of distilled liquor a year—equal to more than two gallons of pure alcohol—along with many gallons more of beer, cider, and wine.

A 1799 ledger from George Washington's Mount Vernon distillery recorded an active business, including the sale of almost 11,000 gallons of whiskey.

Drunkenness wasn't the big worry it would later become, but there were already some concerns. Benjamin Rush, a signer of the Declaration of Independence, former surgeon general of the Continental Army, and maybe the most renowned doctor of the day, published a famous pamphlet in 1784 warning of serious troubles that hard liquor caused drinkers.

Beer, wine, water, and cider were fine, even healthful, he wrote in *An Enquiry into the Effects of Spirituous Liquors upon the Human Body and Their Influence upon the Happiness of Society.* But the "ardent spirits" were another matter. Too much of them seemed to create terrible symptoms, including weakness, vomiting, a bloated belly, tremors in the hands, red flecks in the cheeks, and a "peculiar fullness and flabbiness" in the flesh of the face.

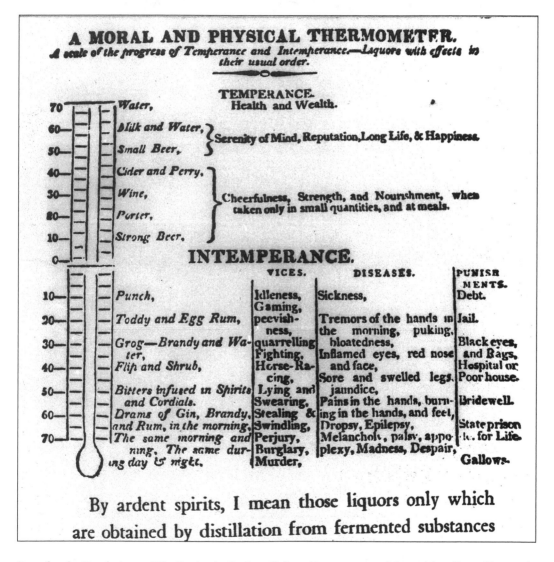

Just after the Revolutionary War, Benjamin Rush spelled out his assessment of the positive effects of beer and wine and the severe damage that hard liquor might cause.

An early temperance illustration, "The Drunkard's Progress," warns of the drinker's steep decline, from the first drink to an early death.

"I do not think it extravagant therefore to repeat here what has been often said, that spirituous liquors destroy more lives than the sword," he wrote. "War has its intervals of destruction—but spirits operate at all times and seasons upon human life."

Rush later devised a "Moral and Physical Thermometer" that displayed how drinking was a quick and slippery slope, starting with tremors and puking from egg rum to the madness and despair of the habitual drunkard. Fearful that drinking would become a major public health problem if it wasn't kept in check, Rush updated and republished his pamphlet several times over the next two decades. With eerie insight, he predicted that the real revolution against alcohol was still more than a century away. "In the year 1915 a drunkard I hope will be as infamous in society as a liar or a thief, and the use of spirits as uncommon in families as a drink made of a solution of arsenic," he wrote a friend in 1788.

Initially, Rush's warnings were largely ignored. But when the young country desperately needed money to pay off war debts in the 1790s, it chose to tax alcoholic beverages, knowing that people loved their liquor so much that they would pay extra to have it. Alexander Hamilton, the secretary of the Treasury, figured that if those taxes also happened to reduce liquor consumption, the nation would be better off, both morally and physically. In 1791, Congress approved an excise tax on hard liquors—the nation's first tax on American goods.

Almost immediately, farmers protested, especially those in western Pennsylvania, North Carolina, and Virginia. For them, the roads to markets were so bad that they couldn't haul all their rye and corn to be sold. So they distilled at least some of it into whiskey, which was less bulky to transport, and they used that whiskey as a form of money, trading it for other goods. These farmers felt particularly singled out and penalized by the taxes, which couldn't be paid in whiskey and which equaled a third of the typical price they received for their distilled spirits.

Western Pennsylvania was particularly whiskey-soaked, and there, tax collectors were sometimes chased down and subjected to painful and often deadly tarring and feathering. Mobs of angry farmers shot holes in the stills and tried to burn the barns and homes of those who complied with the law by paying their taxes. Then, in August 1794, some 7,000 armed protestors demonstrated against the tax and marched through the streets of Pittsburgh.

In the country's first act of national force, President Washington ordered 15,000 troops to the area to stop what became known as the Whiskey Insurrection. Luckily, by the time the troops arrived, the residents had calmed down. There was no further violence, and America's first rebellion was quelled. But for generations after, small still operators would go to great measures to avoid the tax collector.

As settlers moved west to better farming land, whiskey and rum became more plentiful—and cheaper—and at the turn of the nineteenth century, liquor was part of daily American life. In contrast, water might be dirty and milk was perishable and often hard to get. Coffee and tea were expensive. So many families started the day with a glass of whiskey or cider. Workers took breaks at 11 a.m. and again at 4 p.m. for a dramful. Another drink at night helped with digestion and sleep. Babies were given a rum concoction to quiet down, and the sick drank rum and water to perk up. Even children took sips as part of their daily diets.

Abraham Lincoln, born in 1809, recalled that when children "first opened our

In a mid-1800s illustration, parents drink and party to excess at a "gin palace" while their children are neglected.

eyes upon the stage of existence, we found intoxicating liquor, recognized by every body, used by every body, and repudiated by nobody. It commonly entered into the first draught of the infant, and the last draught of the dying man." Doctors prescribed it for all sorts of ailments. "And," he wrote, adding his own emphasis, "to have a rolling or raising, a husking or hoe-down, any where without it was *positively insufferable.*"

In the years between 1800 and 1830, Americans drank more hard liquor than at any other time in their history, each imbibing on average roughly nine gallons a year, or about four gallons of pure alcohol, about twice the level of the previous generation. Beer and wine still had a place at the table, but less so than before.

With more hard drink available, the number of taverns and tippling houses multiplied, as did seedier dramshops and gin houses. Not surprising given the amounts ingested, drunkenness also increased and with it, hardships for families affected by a father's drinking. "Many were greatly injured by it," Lincoln recalled. But the general opinion was that the problems stemmed, he said, not "from the *use* of a *bad thing*, but from the *abuse* of a *very good thing*."

Concerns about that intemperance—or excessive drinking—led to the growth of so-called temperance societies. Members were asked to sign elaborately decorated pledges agreeing to drink only in moderation. Often, people who supported temperance also wanted reform in other areas, calling for an end to slavery, more rights for women, and more education for children.

As the temperance movement began to grow, societies in the 1830s began to discuss a more significant and difficult pledge: an agreement not to drink at all, total abstinence not just from hard liquors, but also from beer, cider, and wine. Those who agreed to live completely "dry" were noted with a "T" by their names on the society's membership rolls, displaying their "total" commitment. In time, those people were known as "teetotalers."

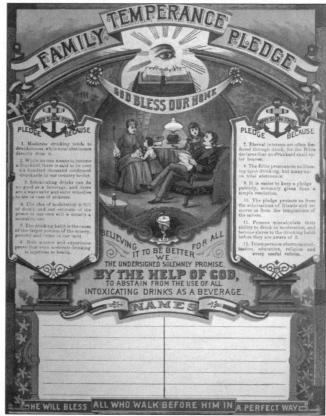

Temperance pledges like this one from the mid-1800s encourage signers to commit in writing to moderation.

Some joined for religious reasons, others because they had personally experienced the tragedy of too much drink. Susan B. Anthony was just six years old in 1826 when her father decided he would never sell liquor again. Daniel Anthony had sold it in a previous store, but changed his mind when he came across a man by the road, frozen to death with a jug in his hand. When he built a new cotton mill and general store in Battenville, New York, he refused to bring in the rum barrels that customers had come to expect, and when he built housing for his workers, he shockingly served only lemonade at the house raising. As a young woman, Susan would first be a crusader for temperance and only later for women to win the right to vote.

Abraham Lincoln himself took a stand in a famous speech in 1842 when he called on fellow citizens to agree to moderate drinking. "Let us make it as unfashionable to withhold our names from the temperance pledge as for husbands to wear their wives' bonnets to church, and instances will be just as rare in the one case as the other," he said. How happy the day will be, he added, "when there shall be neither a slave nor a drunkard on the earth."

Gradually, the temperance movement became part of American culture, prompting all kinds of stories, plays, and speeches aimed at discouraging liquor. At twenty-three, the poet Walt Whitman wrote a novel of the tragic life of an "inebriate," (though he was partly inspired by the money he was offered to do it). The showman P. T. Barnum was an avid temperance speaker. One particularly dramatic novel from the early 1850s, *Ten Nights in a Bar Room*, brimmed with the evils of even a single drink: A little girl named Mary arrives at a saloon to beg her father to come home. But in an exchange between her drunken father, Joe, and the barkeeper, Simon Slade, a glass is hurled that accidentally hits Mary in the head, ultimately killing her. That's only the beginning of the heartbreak and violence; several more lives are shattered before the moral of the tale—that liquor must go—closes the story. *Ten Nights* became a hugely popular temperance play that would be performed off and on for sixty years.

Hoping to influence behavior at a young age, temperance groups also organized children's societies. One of the first was the Cold Water Army, which had an official pledge:

> *We do not think we'll ever drink,*
> *Whiskey or gin, brandy or rum,*
> *Or anything that'll make drunk come.*

In some towns, the little armies met frequently to hear short but stirring speeches, sing temperance songs, and hear stories that warned of the many dangers of drink and the positive effects of plain cold water. When the adults gathered for temperance rallies, the children were often the center of attention, wearing badges with slogans like, "Here we pledge perpetual hate to all things that can intoxicate."

One thousand children joined a march in Baltimore in 1841 wearing red and blue uniforms. The previous year in Duxbury, Massachusetts, one participant remembered, a Fourth of July celebration "drew the entire juvenile population into the ranks" of the Cold Water Army, which "marched into the woods with twice its ordinary numbers, resplendent with flags and many-colored banners, under the escort of a full-fledged band, all palpitating with expectancy."

For nearly two decades, these societies gained members, and hundreds of thousands of people agreed to swear off alcohol. Impressively, by 1850, the amount of hard liquor consumed per person each year dropped by more than half compared with 1830, to about four gallons of spirits, or less than two gallons of pure alcohol. Led by the Oregon Territory and the state of Maine, many towns and several states passed laws outlawing liquor. But as the next decade approached, most of those laws fell by the wayside as Americans came to grips with a much more pressing matter. The fight to end the practice of slavery was ripping the country apart. The Civil War would soon demand the nation's full attention.

CHAPTER 3
HOME DESTROYERS AND DEFENDERS

FROM THE 1860s to the 1870s, as America fought the brutal Civil War and wrestled with the aftermath, the opposition to drinking burbled beneath the surface of American life. Then Dio Lewis, a doctor, editor, educator, and popular lecturer, rolled into Hillsboro, Ohio.

Lewis was an unusual character. He invented the beanbag and imported a wooden dumbbell to help women become more physically active. At a time when women tended the home and rarely spoke out in public, he spoke out for them, arguing for equal rights and campaigning against heavy skirts and bone-crushing corsets. On a temperance lecture tour in 1873, he called for a new role for the ladies: They would be the warriors against the enemy saloons that were popping up across the American landscape.

In the years during and after the Civil War, the drinking issues hadn't gone away; they had just taken a different form. A wave of German immigrants brought both a deep affection for beer and a boom in the number of brewers in many cities, leading some to link the evils of drinking to immigration. Instead of

Women in Mount Vernon, Ohio, brave the cold outside a store to silently protest the sale of liquor.

taverns and lodges, which were the preferred watering holes of the early nineteenth century, saloons sprang up in towns and cities everywhere. Whereas taverns and lodges were hotels and restaurants as well as bars, saloons were primarily drinking places.

By the 1880s, a glut of beer prompted brewers to open up thousands of storefront saloons, which became something like community gathering places. The saloons often offered a free lunch to drinkers, typically cold cuts and salty foods like smoked fish, pretzels, and pork and beans to make the diner thirstier. Men stopped by after work to have a drink while catching up on the day's events, seeing friends, and when the time came, voting. Some of the saloons were elegant and upper crust, but most were rowdy, raucous, and dirty, with sawdust on the floor to hide spills and tobacco juice.

Some women drank, too, but not publicly, typically going to a side entrance to buy beer to take home or buying alcohol from the druggist, who sold liquor or

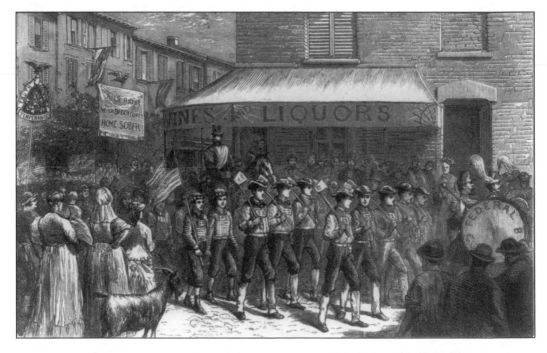

In a magazine illustration, young men march for temperance in a Philadelphia celebration of America's centennial in 1876.

liquor-based cures for almost any kind of ailment—and sometimes just for drinking. With beer and liquor flowing freely from many places, drunkenness and the ugly behavior that went with it became an unpleasant sight in many towns and cities. In Hillsboro, Ohio, a town of just 5,000 people, thirteen saloons, four hotels, and four drugstores sold liquor.

A few days before Christmas 1873, Lewis gave an inspirational temperance speech to a receptive group of Hillsboro women, ending with a moving story about how his own broken-hearted mother had finally fought back against the saloon that sold her husband too much liquor. She and some of her Christian friends banded together and went to that bar to pray for the owner and his customers. Unable to resist—or maybe, unable to conduct business with women praying around them—the saloon had shut down.

Lewis told the crowd they had the same power. Surely the women of Hillsboro could stop the flow of liquor, too, if they "had the same faith." When Lewis asked how many would join such a crusade, at least fifty women stood up.

The next morning, a group of determined women gathered at the Presbyterian church and recruited as their leader Eliza J. Thompson, a mother in her late fifties and the daughter of a former governor who was known for her church and charitable work. Energized by their mission, Mother Thompson led the women two-by-two through a cold and cloudy day toward Dr. William Smith's drugstore. Confronted with a crowd, he signed a "druggists' pledge" that he would no longer sell liquor without a prescription. The ladies then marched to the town's other three stores and won two more signatures.

Christmas Day was reserved for prayer. December 26 brought new snow and new determination. Again the ladies gathered and marched, this time to hotels and saloons where they stopped to pray, sing hymns, and urge the owners to halt their wicked work. On High Street, saloon owner Robert Ward held the heavy door for crusaders and then stood behind the bar to hear from the seventy women dressed in black. Mother Thompson recalled that the saloon keeper began to sweat as the women stated their mission and then asked him to "look upon some of the faces before you, and observe the marks of sorrow, caused by the unholy business that you ply." When one of them said softly, "let us pray," even Mr. Ward went to his knees.

Day after winter day, the Hillsboro women visited the saloons and hotels, until nearly all of them had agreed to close or had been forced to. As word spread of the women's success, other women and children started their own crusades. In Xenia, Ohio, which had more than a hundred saloons, the little students of an all-girls school stood outside a row of saloons each afternoon and sang, "Say, Mr. Barkeeper, has father been here?"

In small towns throughout Ohio, bands of women gathered and prayed in saloons until the owners agreed to close. Sometimes the women were received patiently and politely. Other times, they were threatened, doused with water or beer, spat on, hit with eggs or stones, or, in the bigger cities, beaten by mobs or arrested. Still, the woman's crusade, as it was called, spread to Indiana, across the Midwest, and then to as far away as California and West Virginia.

Temperance was the first major women's political effort and sometimes was seen as a woman's movement.

The women crusaders shuttered thousands of saloons in just a few months. But within the year, many had reopened. Without any new laws to back them or other support, the women were powerless to keep the saloons away.

Even so, something big had happened: A new temperance movement and a new political movement had been born out of the marching and crusading. Freed from the confines of their home lives for the first time, many of those women continued to speak up. In the fall of 1874, representatives from seventeen states gathered in Cleveland, Ohio, and created the Woman's Christian Temperance Union, or WCTU, the nation's first female political powerhouse, an organization that would forever change the way generations looked at drinking, alcohol, and the influence of women.

Initially, the WCTU focused on building a temperance army and drying up America. At its very first convention, the group also committed to build water fountains in busy areas of cities and towns to promote clean water as the preferred drink. Dozens of these fountains were built over many years. In Chicago, children raised $3,000 for a special fountain. In the front, a "little cold water girl" held a bowl where a stream of water overflowed into a trough for horses and a bowl for dogs. On the side, humans could push a button to get clean water.

THE WCTU REALLY took off when Frances Willard became its leader in 1879. A teacher, journalist, and the dean of women at Northwestern University, Willard had big dreams and enormous ambitions for this group, starting with laws that banned drinking. But she called for radical change in other areas, too. She wanted to end public smoking. She was an advocate for more rights for women, fair pay, eight-hour work days, and world peace. Her leadership would make her perhaps the most famous woman in America during the later part of the 1800s.

Willard adopted a catchy slogan, "Home Protection," and argued that women could protect their families from alcohol and other contemporary plagues only if they had some say in their communities. Willard and the WCTU campaigned for a woman's right to vote for local government and the school board, and by 1890—thirty years before all women would be able to vote for president of the United States—nineteen states allowed women to vote in local elections.

Educating children was also part of "Home Protection." New mothers were urged to tie a white ribbon on their babies' wrists, pledging an alcohol-free life.

Children were invited to join Loyal Temperance Legions, which, like the old Cold Water Armies, marched, sang, pledged allegiance to temperance, and heard hair-curling stories about the way alcohol would destroy their families, their homes, and their own bodies and brains.

But where the WCTU really left a lasting imprint on America's children was in schools. Mary H. Hunt, a WCTU member with a particular interest in science, concluded early on that people would accept anti-drinking laws only if generations of students learned that drinking was dangerous. She made it her singular goal that every child would grow up learning that drinking alcohol would be destructive and deadly.

Calling her WCTU division the Department of Scientific Temperance Instruction, Hunt first worked to get temperance textbooks into schools. But then she saw that teachers wouldn't necessarily teach from them. So she turned her attention to state legislatures, campaigning for laws that required schools to specifically teach students the devastating effects of alcohol on their bodies.

COMPLIMENTS OF
GEORGE H. GIES,
16 Monroe Avenue,
DETROIT MICH.

AGAINST PROHIBITION, NO. 3.
The youngster, ruddy with good cheer.
Serenely sips his Lager Beer.

The temperance effort spawned early prohibition skirmishes, and brewers fought back with ads like this one touting the virtues of beer—even for toddlers.

In 1882, Vermont adopted such a law. Michigan followed the next year. In 1885, Congress would pass a law requiring all students in schools under federal control to learn about temperance as part of their "physiology and hygiene" studies. By 1901, every state in the nation had a temperance education law on its books.

For Hunt, however, the laws weren't enough. She wasn't happy with the lessons themselves, and in the late 1880s began adding her own seal of approval to textbooks that presented facts as she saw them. And though the subject was "scientific instruction," often there was very little science at all.

The Child's Health Primer for primary students, published in 1885, was very detailed—and frightening: Describing how grape juice could become wine, the book declared, "This alcohol is a liquid poison. A little of it will harm any one who drinks it; much of it would kill the drinker." Alcohol, it warned, injures the brain and the nerves and can turn muscle to fat. And, the book said, "It changes the person who drinks it. It will make a good and kind person cruel and bad; and will make a bad person worse."

The textbook continued, "The more the drinker takes, the more he often wants, and thus he goes on from drinking cider, wine, or beer, to drinking whiskey, brandy, or rum. Thus drunkards are made."

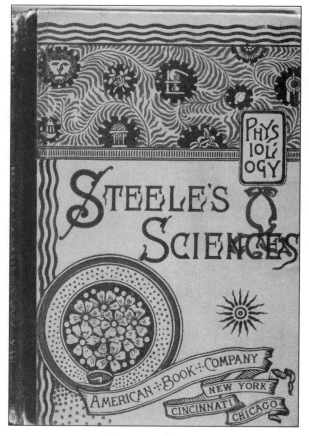

Science textbooks endorsed by the WCTU's Scientific Temperance Division detail the evils and dangers of even a sip of beer or liquor.

In some classes, children were forced to memorize long passages and recite them word for word. Others sang songs and learned anti-alcohol poems. This came from an 1892 primer:

> Apples, ripe apples, we'll pick from the trees,
> But cider—no cider for us, if you please.
> Grapes, purple grapes, for your eating and mine,
> But we'll turn down our glasses where pours the red wine.

Barley, fresh barley, we'll welcome as bread,
But when made into beer it is poison instead.
We'll enjoy all the good things God maketh to grow,
When men change them to poisons, we'll bravely say, "No."

Textbooks for intermediate grades and high schools carried the same messages with more scientific language. To support the lessons, many schoolroom walls were decorated with detailed drawings of the diseased innards of drinkers—the kind of posters that may have led Morris Sheppard to oppose drinking as a young man.

The books, drawings, and downbeat messages were upsetting and unsettling to children whose family members might have a drink or two without any ill effects. (Though the movement still talked about temperance, there was no place at school for moderation, for a single glass of wine or beer with a friend.)

Alcohol, You Can't Fool Me

(Tune: "Yankee Doodle")

1. Alcohol is bad for me,
   It's very bad for you, sir;
   It dulls your brain and hurts your nerves,
   And makes you silly too, sir.

   Chorus:—Alcohol, you can't fool me
            With promises untrue, sir;
            I have need to use my brains
            And keep my senses too, sir.

2. Alcohol impairs your cells;
   Your corpuscles grow weak, sir,
   They cannot carry oxygen;
   Your heart may start to leak, sir.

3. Alcohol breaks down your will,—
   You can't refuse a drink, sir;
   Your conscience deadens down until
   You don't know what you think, sir.
   —ALFREDA POST CARHART

Temperance youth group meetings often included lectures, lessons, and temperance songs put to well-known tunes.

Even more disturbing were the experiments that Hunt and her supporters encouraged teachers to perform. Owen P. White, a writer for *Collier's* magazine, remembered lining up in front of his teacher's desk as a six-year-old in the 1880s. Before her was a jar with a piece of calf brain in a healthy pinkish hue and a glass of alcohol. Demonstrating the potential effect of one on the other, the teacher poured the alcohol in the jar. Quickly, the brain turned a sickly gray. Then, the teacher let them know "that was exactly what would happen to our little brains if we ever got on intimate terms or even dallied with the Demon Rum."

Young Owen was confused. Why would his brain be in his stomach when he drank something like that? Still, twenty-five years later, he vividly remembered both the gruesome sight and the clear message that "alcohol is an excessively dangerous thing to fool with."

Some educators fought back against the WCTU's aggressive teaching methods. The presidents of several famous universities, including Yale, Stanford, Columbia, Cornell, and Vassar, opposed them. A group of scholars said the lessons were "neither scientific, nor temperate, nor instructive." But once in place, the lessons and the books were almost impossible to remove.

After Mary Hunt died in 1906, the WCTU stopped endorsing textbooks. But the temperance education laws and many of the lessons remained for another twenty years. Much would happen in the coming years to lead the country toward prohibition, but the WCTU and Hunt may have laid the most significant foundation of all: They prepared a generation to accept a most unusual constitutional amendment.

CHAPTER 4
A NATION DIVIDES

A S THE NEW CENTURY DAWNED, Carrie Amelia Nation of Medicine Lodge, Kansas, was growing increasingly agitated. In 1880, her state had adopted a constitutional amendment that outlawed the manufacture and sale of any alcoholic beverage. But now, twenty years later, saloons and hotel bars operated as though the law had never existed. Because the owners often paid bribes to local officials, law enforcement simply looked the other way.

Nation, a stout woman in her fifties of about average height, had recently been elected the president of the Barber County WCTU, and she knew the heartbreak of alcohol all too well. When she was nineteen, she had fallen in love with a young doctor over her parents' objections. They courted in secret before she married him two years later. He was the true love of her life, but she realized only after marriage that he was also an alcoholic.

Within months, he was staggering home drunk well into the night, and then, many nights, he failed to come home at all. His medical practice fell apart, and Carrie didn't have enough food.

Carrie Nation, the notorious bar smasher, often wore a white bow of temperance and carried a Bible, believing she was on a mission from God.

She begged the lodge where he drank to turn him away and prayed for his salvation. But finally, pregnant and desperate, she left him and returned to her parents' home. Her beloved husband drank himself to death within the year, leaving her a widow and single mother at twenty-two.

She became a teacher before marrying David Nation, a sometime-minister, farmer, and lawyer. After moving several times, the Nations settled in Medicine Lodge, where Mother Nation helped open a mission school and traveled the county collecting food and clothing for the poor. She trained to be an osteopath, a kind of medical specialist, and helped deliver babies and treat the sick. Deeply religious, she also ministered to jail inmates, whose troubles often seemed to stem from too much drink, even in a state where alcohol was supposed to be banned.

Saloons, like the Bowery in New York, might be dirty and sometimes disorderly, but they also were a haven for the working class.

Bossy, determined, increasingly outspoken, and unwavering in her beliefs—she often snatched cigarettes and cigars from the mouths of smokers and stomped on them—Nation grew more and more angry over her inability to end drinking. As an active WCTU member, she and other Medicine Lodge members had closed down the town's saloons with prayer and insistent demands, much like the Ohio ladies had in the 1870s. But when she protested, wrote politicians, and made other pleas for officials to help close saloons across Kansas, she was ignored. She even tried recruiting the state's governor, a longtime Sunday school teacher, to her cause, but he was too busy "attempting to shame the women of Kansas into abandoning the vice of card-playing."

In June 1900, frustrated and fed up, she sought divine inspiration. She prayed for guidance, telling God that she had run out of ideas. Just before she woke the next morning, she wrote later, she heard the distinct words, "Go to Kiowa," and she had a vision of her hands throwing something, followed by the promise, "I'll stand by you." In her heart, she was certain that she had been commanded to smash saloons. Her life would take a completely new turn.

That afternoon, she filled a box in her buggy with stones, broken bricks, and empty bottles wrapped in paper and set out for Kiowa, Kansas. After spending the night with a friend, she rose early, surprising a saloon keeper and a few customers as she entered the bar with the wrapped rocks and brick pieces stacked on one arm like packages from a store. The saloon keeper recognized the temperance supporter and tried to talk with her, but Mother Nation wasn't interested in chatting. With determination, she began to hurl her brick pieces at windows, mirrors, and bottles, leaving a trail of broken and splintered glass. "I felt invincible," she said later.

When all her weapons were gone, she reloaded, moved down the road to another saloon, and did it again. There, after one brick failed to shatter a mirror, she grabbed a billiard ball from the pool table and launched it toward the mirror, putting a hole in it.

She had ravaged three saloons before the mayor and sheriff confronted her in the street. They considered arresting her—but realized that would only call more attention to the illegal operations in their town. Eventually, they let her go.

Word spread even before she returned to her hometown. Some of her neighbors and fellow temperance workers were angry that she had chosen violence and destruction to make her point. But others in the temperance movement saw her one-woman revolt as a chance to finally make an impression on the powerful saloon owners and politicians.

Nation smashed the mirror and a painting of a nude woman (barely visible in the mirror) during her "hatchetation" of the Carey Hotel.

Mother Nation's next protest would have more consequences—and it would also have far more impact.

Just after Christmas 1900, her husband went to visit his brother, and Nation headed out by train for Wichita, in what would become her signature clothing: a black dress and bonnet, with a large white-ribbon bow at her neck. She carried her husband's heavy cane, and she packed a thick iron rod in her bag—"because I found out by smashing in Kiowa that I could use a rock but once."

Once again, she rose early to start her work. She singled out the bar at the elegant Carey Hotel, known most for its stucco from the Chicago World's Fair, its solid-cherry bar, and its brass spittoons. But what attracted Carrie was a large painting of a nude woman called *Cleopatra at the Bath*, which was hung prominently not because it was artistically special or beautiful, but because the men liked to look at it. To her, this kind of "art," common in many saloons, was a double insult, demeaning to women, and on display in a place that separated mothers from their husbands and sons. When she entered the Carey bar, her first move was to hurl stones at the painting, shattering the glass and tearing the canvas. She then took aim at an expensive mirror and threw stones at bottles and decanters. She pounded on a sideboard with her cane and iron rod.

By 8:30 a.m., she had been arrested, and by evening, she had been charged with malicious destruction of property—even though she argued that the bar itself was illegal. Within hours, news of her mad rampage was buzzing along telegraph wires. The next day, newspapers all the way to New York City carried stories about the Kansas woman who single-handedly tore up a barroom. She was compared to—and she compared herself to—John Brown, the anti-slavery activist (and former Kansas resident) who became a martyr for the abolition cause.

A cartoon depicts the grandmotherly Nation as an oversized bully who leaves barkeepers quivering.

Hundreds of letters and telegrams poured into the Wichita jailhouse, some congratulating and encouraging Mother Nation, others scolding and threatening her. Though she was far from the first female temperance activist to destroy a bar, her timing was just right. By putting a face and a singular action on the liquor fight, she caught the public's imagination. As some praised her and many mocked her and made fun of her, she became the first celebrity of the decades-long movement.

Wichita officials were unsure what to do with their now-famous prisoner, whom critics tried to paint as a mentally unstable old woman. Reluctant to let Mother Nation out on bail, they tried instead to extend her jail stay and make it as unpleasant as possible. Police brought in a mentally ill man who shouted curses constantly and tore at his clothes, placed him in a cell next to her, and then declared he had been exposed to smallpox. As a result, they announced, the jail would be quarantined and no prisoner could leave for three weeks. Just to be sure Mother Nation was truly miserable, the sheriff provided cigarettes to the other prisoners so they could blow smoke her way.

Her supporters went to bat for her, questioning the quarantine and appealing her imprisonment to the Kansas Supreme Court, which ruled in her favor. On January 12, 1901, more than two weeks after her arrest, she was released from jail, more inspired and agitated than ever.

Kansas temperance workers called themselves "Home Defenders" and sold buttons (enlarged here) to raise money for their cause.

Nine days later, with three helpers, Mother Nation destroyed another Wichita saloon, using a hatchet for the first time. Then the group moved to a saloon owned by John Herrig, where they broke the glass windows and much of the glass in the front room, until Herrig approached with a revolver. Putting the gun to Mother Nation's temple, he threatened to blow her brains out. Convinced that he might, the group departed and headed for the Carey Hotel, attracting a crowd that grew to 2,000 people. They were arrested there, and police took the women to the jail, but let them go after they agreed to cease their smashing in Wichita for a time.

With another huge crowd gathering, Mother Nation stopped to preach. Defiantly, she shook her fist and declared, "Men of Wichita, this is the right arm of God and I am destined to wreck every saloon in your city!" But keeping her promise to give Wichita a break, she and her helpers set out for the train station to continue their wreckage in a town called Enterprise.

The sheriff of Wichita, hearing of the new plans, tried to arrest her again. But the small man was little match for this physically strong and strong-minded midwestern woman. She slapped him across the face and followed that by "taking hold of his ears with both of her hands and wringing them viciously," according to a news account. A policeman had to rescue the sheriff. Mother Nation earned more time in the Wichita jail.

Released again a couple of days later, she headed to Enterprise, where her violence was met with more violence. There a saloon keeper's irate wife gave her a black eye, and she was beaten with horsewhips by others.

Nation sold thousands of small hatchet pins like this one (enlarged here) to fund her crusade.

Undaunted, she marched to the capital, Topeka, in February to continue what she now called her "hatchetation." There, she made a special plea to high school students, urging them "to grab up a rock and smash up the glass doors and windows of these hell holes." Those who did, she promised, would win "undying fame and place yourself on the side of God and humanity." Few took her up on the offer, however.

While she was preaching on a street corner there, a store owner dropped a handful of little pewter hatchet pins in her hand, leftovers from Washington's Birthday, and urged her to sell them to help pay her fines. She would end up selling thousands of tiny hatchet pins over the years, as well as "Home Defender" buttons—sales that would not only pay her fines, but also fund her travels, support charities, and take care of her in retirement.

Nation also visited the state legislature in Topeka to give lawmakers an earful about her crusade. "A good solid vote is the best thing in the world with which to smash the saloons," she told them. "But you wouldn't give me the vote, so I had to use a rock!"

Altogether, Carrie Nation's intense "hatch-etation" lasted less than a year. But in that short time, she became world famous. Others imitated her smashing in the United States and abroad. In an early movie, *The Kansas Saloon Smashers*, inventor Thomas A. Edison satirized her, presenting the saloons as clean and healthy places attacked by uptight women because a few lowlifes visited them. She became a well-known lecturer, took roles in temperance plays like *Ten Nights in a Bar Room,* and was occasionally arrested for threatening or challenging authorities. From time to time, she would break some whiskey bottles or throw a glass to make her point. In 1903, realizing that her father had misspelled her name in the family Bible, she took to spelling it Carry A. Nation, a symbol, she thought, of the important job God had given her to destroy the saloon.

Mother Nation died in 1911, several months after collapsing at her last speech, saying weakly, "I have done what I could." While staying staunchly committed to her mission,

After her initial saloon smashings, Nation toured the country as a lecturer, drawing huge crowds.

she had been jailed a total of twenty-two times. Early biographers painted her as half-crazed, a troubled woman from a family with a history of mental illness. That was a gross overstatement. In many ways, though, she came off as a caricature—a scolding and angry religious fanatic dressed in black—and that image of prohibition's female supporters would linger for many years. Through controversial and unconventional methods, she put the spotlight on the saloon business and inspired followers, perhaps doing more to raise the visibility of the movement than any other single person.

But while Mother Nation could sway public opinion, she and her female followers still couldn't bring about concrete, permanent change. For that, they needed real political muscle—and votes. It just so happened that while the WCTU and radicals like Nation were drawing attention to the issue, a group of men were building a political powerhouse unlike any the country had ever seen.

CHAPTER 5
WAR!

I N 1893, Howard H. Russell, a Congregationalist minister, founded the Anti-Saloon League in Oberlin, Ohio, with a mission to save people from "the evils of the drink habit and . . . the debauching curse of the drink traffic."

Russell and his small group of like-minded men had a single goal: to outlaw saloons and drinking as well. Like the WCTU, they believed in agitation, or rallying public opinion to their cause. But then they followed up with a push for legislation and enforcement. To fund their efforts, they raised money through churches, asking congregants to pledge contributions of 25¢, or $1 a month.

With that money, the league hired advocates to lobby for public and political support. If the league couldn't win a local election to outlaw saloons, it recruited and supported elected officials who would support new laws. Charging that the saloon was the creator of sin in society, it began to march town by town, county by county, and then state by state, from Ohio to the rest of the country.

For many poorer Americans, new immigrants, and the working class, the complaints of the WCTU

To rally supporters, prohibition advocates often looked to young people, like these Corbin, Kentucky, children, to help drive home their anti-liquor message.

and the Anti-Saloon League were hard to understand. The saloon was often the workingman's community center, a place to see friends, unwind, and catch up on the news of the day, even if he drank a lot doing so. Even the Chicago reformer Jane Addams, who later would support prohibition, noted that the saloon "offers the working people the only kind of social relaxation they have."

A young boy "rushes the growler," carrying a beer pail home, in an image by documentary photographer Jacob Riis.

Women, for the most part, weren't welcome in the saloon proper, but a family entrance was like today's take-out counter. At a time before canned drinks or reliable refrigeration, women and children would bring in the family's beer pail or jug to the family entrance to be filled for a dime, about the price of a pint, though the quantity was much more than that. Many boys and teens made pocket money by picking up buckets at the factories at lunchtime and carrying them on long poles to the saloon to be filled. The job was known as "rushing the growler." (The name may have come from the sound the pail made when the lid bounced on top of it.)

Behind the scenes, these thriving businesses were also awash in influence and corruption. Saloons often were located near factories, and some acted as banks, cashing customers' paychecks while also relieving them of a substantial part of their earnings each week. In most places, saloons were supposed to close on Sundays, but local proprietors often opened anyway because Sunday was such a profitable day.

Powerful brewers typically owned the buildings and the furniture, charging the proprietors high rents. They also controlled the price of beer, and profits were slim for the saloon operator. Brewers urged the saloons to push beer and liquor, and even to encourage young boys to take up the habit. "We must create the appetite for liquor in growing boys" to ensure future customers, a delegate to a meeting of the Retail Liquor Dealers' Association of Ohio once said. "Nickels expended in treats to boys now will return in dollars to your tills after the appetite has been formed."

Local police often received special payments to protect saloons or let them open on Sundays. To make ends meet, some saloon keepers ran gambling operations in the back rooms or cheated their customers by watering down liquor or selling cheap imitations for the price of fancy brands. In 1908, an estimated 3,000 brewers and distillers churned out beer and spirits for more than 100,000 legal saloons, with another 50,000 or so operating without licenses. Half of the populations of Boston and Chicago visited a saloon every day.

The idea that a small group of strong-willed, church-going temperance advocates could whip these influential brewers and saloon owners seemed preposterous, if not impossible. For years, a determined Prohibition Party had put up anti-alcohol candidates, with little success. And when the Anti-Saloon League was founded, almost no states prohibited liquor sales.

But by first winning over local politicians and working up from there, the Anti-Saloon League gradually began to build a political base. By 1906, more than thirty states had adopted laws that gave towns or counties the right to vote themselves dry, and hundreds had done so.

Then, realizing that local votes didn't matter much if people could just drive down the road and get a drink, the league turned its attention to state governments. By early 1908, the *Washington Post* reported, more than one-third of the U.S. population—some 33 million people—were living under so-called prohibition laws, either local or statewide. Even so, the newspaper noted, tax revenues from liquor sales nationwide continued to grow, indicating that people still were drinking at will.

By 1912, the years of identifying and supporting dry candidates began to show some results. Though several states had gone dry, anyone who wanted a drink could bring liquor in from another state or order it by mail. The league and its supporters asked the U.S. Congress to ban liquor imports into states that prohibited liquor sales.

Both prohibition advocates and the beer and liquor industries bombarded their congressmen with telegrams and letters. To the surprise of many, Congress in 1913 sided with the prohibitionists, banning mail-order sales.

Though the law passed, it was never officially enforced, and some saw that as a failure. But the Anti-Saloon League saw something much more significant: It had votes. And suddenly, a much bigger goal—a national law—seemed less farfetched.

Despite their strong tactics, prohibition advocates genuinely wanted to protect children, such as these youngsters sharing a bottle, a cigarette, and some bread, captured by documentary photographer Lewis Hine.

Fresh off its big Washington win, the Anti-Saloon League and the WCTU began to link arms to pursue a broader goal—and to carry out an unprecedented political attack. "The smell of battle was in the air; the clouds of the storm were rolling in from the West and South," wrote Wayne B. Wheeler, the league's top lawyer and lobbyist, referring to growing support in those states.

At its annual convention in November 1913, the Anti-Saloon League marked its twenty-fifth year with celebration. Toward the end of the session, the governor of Indiana, J. Frank Hanly, took the podium to declare the group's audacious goal: "national annihilation" of liquor traffic through an amendment to the U.S. Constitution, a change that would require both Congress's approval and the support of three-fourths of the states.

"For a moment there was silence, tense and deep," Mr. Wheeler wrote later. "Then the convention cut loose. With a roar as wild as the raging storm outside, it jumped to its feet and yelled approval."

In many parts of the country, the news was seen as just another group of moralists promoting an agenda. But some sirens sounded. The *Los Angeles Times* reported that the league had launched perhaps "the greatest attack ever made on property" in the United States, threatening to shut every brewery, distillery, and saloon. The newspaper noted that the group was clever, with friends in high places and a growing war chest of donations.

On the other side of the country, the *Boston Daily Globe* reported that prominent Democrats in the U.S. House of Representatives were nervous about the strength of the political support—and the number of votes—the prohibition groups had. "The situation is tense enough," the newspaper said, "to cause cold chills to creep up and down the spines of the Democratic leaders in both houses."

When the WCTU and the Anti-Saloon League actually gathered on December 10, 1913, to put a proposed constitutional amendment in the hands of Senator Morris Sheppard of Texas, however, most large newspapers hardly treated the event as news. "Anti-Rum Army at Capitol," the *New York Times* said, giving the effort just five paragraphs on page five.

After the amendment was introduced in Congress, the Anti-Saloon League got to work—but not in Washington. The proposed amendment needed to wend its way through the legislative process. The league wanted to be sure its amendment had enough votes when the right moment arrived.

The day after the march, league leaders met to map out an unprecedented battle plan. They would campaign for "dry" congressmen in every district where they had a reasonable chance. The league sent word to its supporters nationwide: "Open fire on the enemy." And using every tool of democracy, they did.

Supporters were urged to send letters, telegrams, and petitions to their representatives. Wheeler, the league's chief lobbyist, reported that "they rolled in by tens of thousands, burying Congress like an avalanche."

An estimated 20,000 mostly volunteer speakers took every opportunity to lecture at churches and public gatherings about the evils of saloons and drink. As the campaign grew, up to 50,000 speakers blanketed the country, preaching the anti-alcohol message in what Wheeler called "a vocal army storming the enemy trenches."

The league already had eight active printing presses in Westerville, Ohio, that had pumped out more than forty tons of temperance literature a month in 1912. But the presses were cranked up further, turning out books, magazines, pamphlets, Sunday school lessons, posters, and fliers in stunning quantities. New

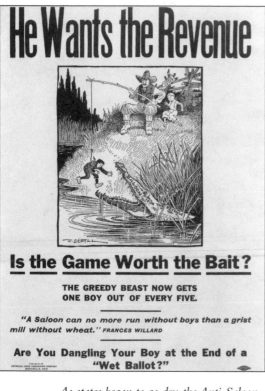

He Wants the Revenue

Is the Game Worth the Bait?

THE GREEDY BEAST NOW GETS
ONE BOY OUT OF EVERY FIVE.

"A Saloon can no more run without boys than a grist mill without wheat." FRANCES WILLARD

Are You Dangling Your Boy at the End of a "Wet Ballot?"

As states began to go dry, the Anti-Saloon League turned up the printing presses, churning out anti-liquor posters like the ones above and to the right.

monthly and weekly publications were added, and at times, the presses ran three shifts, twenty-four hours a day, to churn out railcar-loads of material that would be mailed to individuals or delivered to churches and other temperance groups.

The singular message was familiar, but still powerful: The saloon must go and so should "The Great Destroyer," alcohol, which ruined health, broke up marriages, and led to general economic ruin. Only by outlawing drink, the messages continued, would America rid itself of crime, mental illness, and poverty. Without saloons, men would work harder, families would be happier, and more young people would attend high school and college. America would be a stronger and more successful country.

The sheer volume of propaganda called more attention to the message, while dividing Americans. To the middle and upper classes, who could afford to buy their own liquor and bring it home, the saloons were nothing but a breeding ground for riffraff and crime. In the South, whites fought for regulations to keep alcohol away from blacks. The campaign highlighted the nation's differences, pitting rural Americans against city dwellers, the middle class against the working class, native-born Americans against immigrants, race against race, and eventually, faith against faith, as some Protestants challenged wine used by Catholics and Jews.

Thirty-Six States Can Stop This By Constitutional Amendment

—Good Housekeeping

The 2,000,000 children in bondage to toil is an outrage against our civilization, but the millions enslaved by the licensed liquor traffic is the foulest blot upon our nation's honor.

Excessive Death-Rate In Drinking Homes Cost 2,407 Children Their Lives

(Statistics, 19,519 children in 5,726 families.)

SERIES G. No. 21.

Changing times, coupled with years of temperance education, also made the prohibition argument easier to absorb. Saloons grew less popular as more employers frowned on drinking during the workday and automobiles allowed people to get around more easily. Picnic grounds and early movie theaters encouraged young men and women to do things together. Dance halls became an alternative to saloons. Women were drinking socially more often—but at their own dinner tables, not in gin joints. Men listened to concerns that drinking was bad for their young.

The momentum began to shift. But powerful brewers, distillers, and saloon owners arrogantly ignored the winds of change blowing in far from Washington. Some local saloon owners even thumbed their noses at the "drys," framing and hanging the Anti-Saloon League's most frightful posters on their walls to amuse their customers. The brewers and distillers might have stopped the prohibition movement cold, many experts believe, if they had simply cleaned up or even shut down saloons, rather than continuing to pursue the profits from them.

Instead, brewers and distillers fought back with a propaganda campaign of their own. The United States Brewers' Association raised money from its members and used the funds to plant anti-prohibition stories in newspapers and magazines. State brewery organizations led their own campaigns, supporting local newspapers with advertising.

In a position that would grow increasingly unpopular, the brewers and distillers also generally opposed a woman's right to vote, assuming that women supported prohibition. They also secretly made improper contributions to friendly politicians and sometimes resorted to bribery. In 1914 and 1915, brewer associations in Pennsylvania and Texas were charged with manipulating both liquor and suffrage elections, among other charges, and were assessed fines.

Both sides spent hundreds of thousands of dollars. But in the 1914 election, the Anti-Saloon League won more seats than it expected—though not quite enough to pass a constitutional amendment.

Both sides redoubled their efforts and their campaigns. "All the energy we put into the 1914 election campaign boiled and bubbled with hotter fire in the campaign of 1916," Wheeler said. "We laid down such a barrage as candidates for Congress had never seen before."

With so much attention on the subject, the issue began to play a pivotal role in the politics of the day. The drys demanded that people running for just about any office declare whether they were wet or dry—there was no in-between. Wets, by contrast, were often moderate drinkers who preferred to leave the prohibition decision to individual communities. As a group, they weren't organized politically. And because liquor was widely available even in areas that were dry, many people may have simply believed that prohibition would never happen.

They may also have been distracted. While drys were waging a moral war on American soil, a real and increasingly deadly war was spreading across Europe.

What seemed to be a skirmish in the summer of 1914 exploded within months into the Great War. By the end of the year, Russia, France, Great Britain, Canada, and others were battling Germany and Austria-Hungary in bloody

Opposing billboards in Columbus, Ohio, urge voters to take different sides; a sample ballot recommends specific votes on prohibition, but is silent on women's suffrage.

combat involving nearly every country in Europe and millions of men. The story took over the front pages of American newspapers, pushing prohibition news inside—including the fact that ten states adopted prohibition laws between 1915 and 1916, bringing the total number of states that limited liquor sales to nineteen.

While the war overseas drained the resources of America's closest allies, at home it gave the drys the crucial ammunition to finish their own battle. First, Americans began to reject anything German as tainted, including the nation's more than 1,200 mostly German-American breweries. The drys portrayed any support for beer or brewers as truly unpatriotic. Then there was a more practical problem: American allies were desperately short of food. Several nations banned or cut back the manufacture of alcoholic beverages to preserve grains and open up railcars for transporting other much-needed items. America, the drys argued, needed to do the same.

In the fall 1916 elections, the league and other prohibition supporters channeled all their efforts toward winning statewide races. In the national election, President Woodrow Wilson, the Democratic nominee, and Charles Evans Hughes, the Republican nominee, were locked in a tight race, and neither supported prohibition. On election night, Hughes appeared to have the lead, prompting several newspapers, including the *New York Times*, to initially report that he had won.

That night, state Anti-Saloon League workers tallied their own results—and realized they were the real winners. Enough prohibition supporters had been elected to the Senate and House of Representatives to drive a constitutional amendment through Congress. "Many hours before the country knew whether Hughes or Wilson had triumphed, the dry workers throughout the nation were celebrating our victory," Wayne Wheeler, the league's lawyer, wrote.

By 1917, America and President Wilson could no longer sit on the sidelines of the war. In March 1917, the president called a session of the new Congress to declare war on Germany, saying, "The world must be made safe for democracy." A military draft was started in May, and the first soldiers landed in France in the summer. A wartime food-control bill outlawed the use of grains and other foods to make hard liquor, taking effect that fall, and later, laws would require beer to be watered-down to 3.2 percent alcohol, dubbed "near beer."

Sometime in June of that year, the rotund Senator Boies Penrose of Pennsylvania lumbered up to the slight Texas senator, Morris Sheppard, on the Senate floor with a proposition. The constitutional amendment that Sheppard first proposed in 1913 had been languishing in Penrose's committee, despite growing support for prohibition. But, Penrose told him, he wouldn't oppose its moving to a Senate vote if Sheppard would give in on one point.

"What's the change?" Sheppard asked.

A deadline, Penrose explained. In addition to winning approval from Congress, a constitutional amendment had to be approved by at least three-fourths of the states—thirty-six to be exact. Penrose insisted that the states approve the amendment within six years—or the amendment would die.

Sheppard was on the spot. No amendment had ever had to meet this kind of artificial deadline.

A campaign button (enlarged here) urges voters to support a prohibition law.

"I had to think fast," Sheppard said. "I knew that Penrose was trying to play a trick on me." The wets figured that six years wasn't long enough for all those state legislatures to act.

"Half a dozen years seemed an awfully short time to me. It did to everybody," Sheppard said.

But, he said, "I had to take a chance." So, he agreed.

As promised, the bill moved out of committee and Sheppard finally introduced it on the Senate floor in late July. After decades of lectures and lobbying, piles upon piles of pamphlets and temperance publications, and one of the shrewdest political campaigns ever executed, the actual vote was almost anticlimactic.

After a mere thirteen hours of debate over three days, the Senate approved the constitutional amendment, 65 to 20.

That night, wets in Washington celebrated, sure that at least thirteen of the nation's forty-eight states would reject this amendment, blocking its enactment. Some of Sheppard's friends accused him of being a traitor. With America embroiled in the Great War, they reasoned, state legislatures would be too busy to mess with a prohibition amendment.

Sheppard worried that his friends might be right. "To speak the truth, I was heartsick myself that night," he said later.

The fight moved to the House. In a compromise, the House agreed that the amendment wouldn't go into effect until a year after it was ratified. In exchange, the drys would have seven years instead of six to win over the states.

On December 17, the House approved the new amendment by a vote of 282 to 128, allowing it to be submitted, in Senator Sheppard's words, "as a Christmas present to the American people." It was a fairly wordy gift, reading:

"After one year from the ratification of this article, the manufacture, sale, or transportation of intoxicating liquors within, the importation thereof into, or the exportation thereof from the United States and all territory subject to the jurisdiction thereof for beverage purposes is hereby prohibited."

Sheppard, always an optimist, predicted that the necessary states would ratify the amendment in three years. He was too pessimistic. The state legislatures were the Anti-Saloon League's home field, and the opposition had no organized defense. Within four weeks, the Mississippi legislature ratified the new amendment without a word of debate. In the days after that, Virginia, Kentucky, and South Carolina followed. Approvals rolled through one state after another. In January 1919, not quite thirteen months after Congress acted, Nebraska became the thirty-sixth state to vote for ratification, officially adding the Eighteenth Amendment to the U.S. Constitution. Ultimately every state but Rhode Island and Connecticut would approve the amendment.

The new law would take effect in 1920—just as the Woman's Christian Temperance Union had hoped back in 1913.

But there was one more step—and one more hurdle to leap.

Congress needed to come up with specifics, to spell out, for instance, what an "intoxicating" beverage actually was, as well as penalties and consequences if the amendment was violated. Representative Andrew Volstead led the effort, and the resulting bill became commonly known as the Volstead Act. Some legislators had hoped to keep wine and beer—or at least near beer—legal, but the drys wouldn't hear of it. Instead, any beverage with an alcohol content of more than one-half of one percent was considered intoxicating, a much stiffer definition than many expected. After much debate, individuals were allowed to keep liquor in their own homes, for their own use, and exceptions

Members of the American Federation of Labor rally against prohibition in 1919, but the efforts are too little, too late.

Andrew Volstead pushed for much more stringent rules than many expected, effectively outlawing beer and wine as well as hard liquor; he was defeated in the next election.

were made for wine used for religious purposes and alcohol for medicine. But that was about it.

The Volstead Act passed in October 1919 and also included measures for enforcing wartime prohibition—although the war had ended almost a year before. To the surprise of many, an ill President Wilson, propped up in bed following a stroke, took issue with that. He vetoed the bill, exercising his power to reject it.

Though the veto "hit Congress like a crack of lightening," legislators didn't waste any time responding. To override a president's veto, two-thirds of both the House and the Senate had to vote for the act. Within two hours, the House voted overwhelmingly in favor; the Senate did so the next day.

Stung by the strict regulations of the Volstead Act and the stark reality of what was ahead, the wets, especially in big cities, cried foul. They were way too late.

The drys were gleeful. Crime would soon disappear, jails would close, and hospitals would lose patients. Families would flourish and America would prosper as never before.

Those were the expectations. The reality was something else altogether.

CHAPTER 6

DRY!

Exactly one minute after January 16, 1920, became January 17, daily life in America was immediately changed.

Once the Eighteenth Amendment to the U.S. Constitution became law, ordinary events like taking a bottle of wine to a friend's house, sipping a drink in public, or selling a beer were now illegal from coast to coast, punishable by up to six months of jail time and a fine up to $1,000.

To prepare for the death of King Alcohol, the nation's drinkers had been busy. Officially, the sale and manufacture of hard liquor had been illegal under wartime prohibition since the summer of 1919. But that particular law had been loosely enforced, and since it didn't outlaw transportation or possession of alcohol outside one's home, people had taken to carrying their booze with them, in bottles or flasks. As the date for the constitutional amendment and its more severe penalties approached, all of the bottles and jugs stored in restaurants, offices, bars, old liquor stores, and country clubs had to go—either to government warehouses, or more likely, to safe spots at home or in the

Prohibition Bureau agents are surrounded by crates of whiskey in the hold of a ship seized by the Coast Guard.

homes of trusted friends and neighbors, the only places where liquor could be legally held.

In Boston, the "population appeared to join in one wild scramble . . . to get its alcohol possessions under cover before the fatal hour," the *Boston Daily Globe* reported on January 17. "All day long, automobiles, taxicabs, trucks, and vehicles of all descriptions were in the greatest demand, while pedestrians and homeward-bound suburbanites were loaded with bundles." In St. Paul, Minnesota, neighbors used wheelbarrows, wagons, and sleds to cart home cases of liquor that were nearly given away by wholesalers. In San Francisco, sidewalks were crowded with men lugging suitcases and boxes. In New York, even baby carriages were brought into service.

While it was illegal to sell liquor, it wasn't illegal to buy it or drink it at home. Prices of available bottles shot up in the "undercover" market. Closed and shuttered liquor stores seemed to be doing brisk business out the back door. For drinkers who had frequented restaurants and bars, however, the last minutes of legal alcohol made for a poor party on January 16. Many patrons dressed in black and brought their own booze, and one New York City restaurant gave out miniature caskets as souvenirs. Police and other authorities threatened to seize any glass or bottle on any table as soon as the law went into effect, prompting most public places to shut their doors and turn out the lights by 11:45 p.m. As a result, most final toasts and celebrations took place ahead of time.

Though many states already were dry, prohibition advocates threw their own postwar victory parties.

In New Jersey, drys celebrated with a banquet. In Washington, D.C., they attended a late-night church service and cheered a rousing speech from noted orator (and dry) William Jennings Bryan. In Norfolk, Virginia, the always theatrical Reverend Billy Sunday, a professional baseball player turned evangelist, shared strong words at an elaborate funeral for the mythical "John Barleycorn," a slang term for whiskey, that drew 10,000 viewers.

"Good-bye John," he said. "You were God's worst enemy; you were hell's best friend." He continued, "The reign of tears is over. The slums will soon be only a memory. We will turn our prisons into factories and our jails into storehouses and corncribs. Men will walk upright now, women will smile, and the children will laugh. Hell will be forever rent."

As the drys enjoyed their hard-won victory, others wrestled with how to adjust to the new era. Librarians in Springfield, Massachusetts, and New Haven, Connecticut, decided to pull off the shelves any books describing how to make alcohol. Librarians in New York and San Francisco chose to leave the books in place.

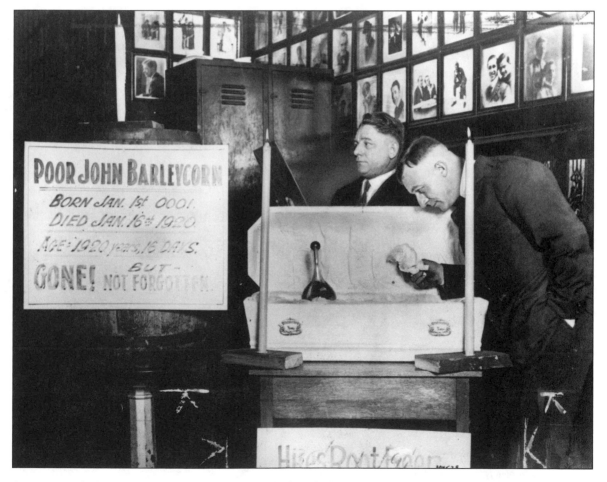

In ceremonies both serious and playful, wets mourned the loss of John Barleycorn, a nickname for liquor.

Brewers like Anheuser-Busch began selling milk and ice cream, as well as a nonalcoholic beer, and others simply closed. In New York, the Hotel Knickerbocker and the Manhattan Hotel, the creators, respectively, of the dry martini and the Manhattan cocktail, shut their doors after their bar business dried up. Fancy restaurants, particularly French-inspired ones, which relied on wine for cooking as well as drinking, went out of business, replaced by an explosion of coffee shops and sandwich outlets.

Some police cracked down: In California, five wine makers were fined for failing to get permits for wines they owned, even though they claimed their holdings—of up to 850 gallons—were for "personal use." For a few months, hospital administrators reported fewer patients with severe drinking problems, and police arrested fewer drunken citizens.

The drys were so convinced that changing the law would automatically change behavior that fairly little thought was put into enforcement of the new amendment. Congress set aside just $2 million for the new Prohibition Bureau, the government office charged with enforcing the law.

Some speakeasies operated in the open, some were completely hidden, and some included peepholes on the door for checking out potential customers.

But the sober behavior was short lived. While the law had changed, the demand for drinks hadn't. In a matter of months, drinking moved from bars and restaurants to the home, where individuals enjoyed their stockpiled liquor. Stores sprang up selling kettles, yeast, grains, and other supplies for distilling your own liquor or brewing your own beer.

Then, in a fairly short time, illegal liquor, beer, and wine became more readily available in all kinds of ways. Every little loophole in the law was exploited. Doctors could write prescriptions for alcohol as medicine, and some did so to an extreme. Priests and rabbis could buy wine for their worshippers, and some purchased extra and sold it for profit. A rabbi in Los Angeles, however, quit after his congregants demanded too much. "They kept calling for wine, wine, and more wine," said Rabbi B. Gardner, who saw his synagogue grow from 180 members to nearly 1,200 members in just over a year. "I refused to violate the law to please them."

Homemade brews were secretly concocted in the cities, and moonshine was manufactured in hidden rural areas. In one particularly embarrassing example, a still capable of making 130 gallons of whiskey a day was found in September 1920 on a Texas farm owned by Senator Morris Sheppard, the author of the prohibition amendment. Though the still was later traced to a cousin, the news implied that even the law's author and biggest supporter didn't take it seriously.

Illegal liquor from Canada and Europe began to flow over America's borders. One of the early rumrunners was a former boat-builder named William McCoy, who realized that he could put his passion for sailing to work running liquor from the Bahamas to the New York area. He earned enough in his first few runs to buy a bigger boat, capable of carrying 5,000 cases of rye and whiskey, bringing him $50,000 a trip.

When too many others crowded the business in the Bahamas, he moved his base to St. Pierre and Miquelon, small French islands near Newfoundland, where he would load his ship with Canadian whiskey or French brandy and pretend to head to the Bahamas. Instead, the ship would stop some distance off the coast of the northeastern United States and pass its load on to small motorboats, which would take it to land.

By the mid-1920s, the business was so strong at St. Pierre that rumrunners were building special boats that were capable of holding 25,000 cases. Huge warehouses sprouted along the waterfront. Residents were making so much money that an auto dealer opened up on the island, even though its longest road was only four miles.

McCoy had such a reputation for honest dealings and good, pure liquor that his booze was known as "the real McCoy." Some people think the expression came from him, though it probably predated prohibition by several decades.

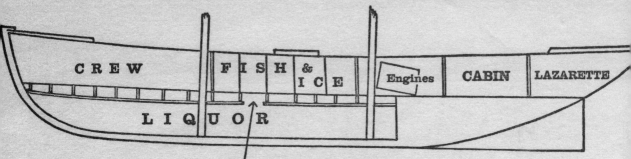

Hatch concealed by cement

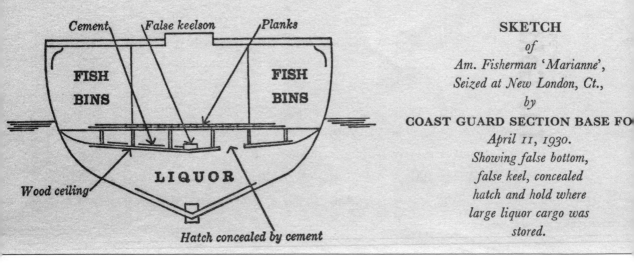

Cement   False keelson   Planks

FISH BINS   FISH BINS

Wood ceiling

LIQUOR

Hatch concealed by cement

SKETCH
of
Am. Fisherman 'Marianne',
Seized at New London, Ct.,
by
COAST GUARD SECTION BASE FO
April 11, 1930.
Showing false bottom,
false keel, concealed
hatch and hold where
large liquor cargo was
stored.

A sketch of a ship captured by the Coast Guard shows how the vessel's hold was modified so that liquor could be smuggled into U.S. waters.

As the once-legal saloons closed, illegal bars, nightclubs, and cabarets began to open up and multiply. In the East, these bars were often called "speakeasies," derived from an old Irish term for illicit bars where patrons should be quiet and "speak easy"—both in the bar and about it—so as not to attract attention. In the Midwest, these were more commonly called "blind pigs" or "blind tigers," a nickname from an old trick to get around the temperance laws that forbade selling alcohol. Instead, sellers sold a chance to look at an imaginary "blind tiger" or "blind pig" for, say, a dime—and then provided an alcoholic drink "for free" along with it.

Leroy Ostransky was just two years old when his dad opened an illegal saloon in New York City in 1920. Growing up, he understood that the bar was the family business, and he came to know it well.

His father Sharkey ran a saloon that was much like the ones from previous decades, long and narrow, with sawdust on the floor, a brass railing along the bar, and heavy swinging doors. In midtown Manhattan, the bars and cabarets were swankier, catering to the upper crust with singers and dancing girls. In Greenwich Village, frequented by college students, the bars might be decorated like a pirate's lair or a pretend jail cell. In Harlem, where African American writers, artists, and musicians were nurturing an artistic renaissance, nightclubs and speakeasies brimmed with a new, exciting sound called jazz. Many of the clubs broke racial barriers by attracting both blacks and whites, though the famous Cotton Club featured black entertainers but had only white customers.

Sharkey served the working class around his East River neighborhood, primarily Irish, Italian, and other immigrants who worked on the piers and in the nearby warehouses and who drank their liquor straight, with maybe some water or ginger ale to wash it down.

Leroy Ostransky poses for one of his few childhood photos, on his bar mitzvah at thirteen.

Keeping the bar stocked was a constant challenge, complicated by the need to always be ready for a possible visit by Prohibition Bureau agents.

A few times a week, trucks delivered "legal" beer, which had an alcohol content of less than one-half of one percent. Sharkey then would inject pure alcohol to make it far more potent—and popular.

For the saloon's regulars, Leroy helped his mother make a cheap homemade whiskey. Always, they began by bolting the front door to prevent unexpected guests. Then, together, they hoisted a five-gallon can of pure grain alcohol,

In a scene that was repeated many times in the 1920s, law enforcement officials pour an illegal brew into the sewer.

poured some into a metal pot, and added water to dilute it. Leroy's mother bought the cans of alcohol several times each week from a local druggist, who stocked it, supposedly for medical purposes.

The two would add a little oil of rye, glycerin, and burnt sugar for flavoring and color, creating quick imitation whiskey. (Made in smaller quantities in the bathtub, because the tall bottles wouldn't fit in the sink, these concoctions often were called "bathtub gin.") Leroy and his mother would siphon the mix into bottles and paste on labels that named their home brew as "Rewco."

Sharkey's best customers got real whiskey, which came from government warehouses to druggists who could sell it to those who could provide a doctor's prescription. Leroy remembered that his local pharmacist "not only *accepted* forged prescriptions, but he *sold* forged prescriptions." Sharkey used to sell the good stuff for 60¢ a shot, but then decided it would be easier to make change if he charged 50¢. His wife took on the job of watering down the real whiskey so he could cut the price.

To keep the local police happy, Sharkey sent cash each week to the commander of his local precinct, as well as to his regular officer. In exchange, they would tell him when they planned their regular monthly arrests, which were simply a part of the prohibition game. "You made it easy for them; you played along; you didn't resist," Leroy recalled. In fact, when the arrest time came, Sharkey left an open bottle of whiskey on the bar, so no one had to go through cabinets or rip apart the plumbing looking for illegal drinks. Caught red-handed, Sharkey would be taken downtown, where a judge would fine him $25 or $50. Within hours, he'd be back at work, visiting and laughing with customers.

His real fear, though, was the unscheduled "pinch," the visit from federal agents who played a different game. Those agents, if they weren't just out for a bribe, were a serious threat. If they found any whiskey at all, they could padlock the front door for a year without even taking the owner to trial. That would put the whole family out of business, maybe forever.

Two New York agents in particular made their names and faces famous with their determination—and creativity—in shutting down places like Sharkey's. Isadore Einstein, known as Izzy, was barely scraping by as a postal clerk in 1920 when he saw the government was hiring about 1,500 new prohibition agents nationwide. The pay, roughly $2,000 a year (or less than $25,000 in today's dollars), was a modest income but more than he was earning.

When he went to apply, however, the chief agent was skeptical. Izzy was forty years old, bald, and at 5 feet, 5 inches tall and more than 200 pounds, very round around the middle. "I must say," the chief told him, "you don't look much like a detective."

But Izzy was a natural salesman and he convinced the chief that he knew something about people and how to win them over, which might prove useful in a business where trust mattered. Many speakeasies required patrons to give secret passwords to get in. Other places were more physically open, like Sharkey's, but bartenders often refused to serve liquor to someone they didn't know and trust. Izzy convinced the chief that maybe a man who didn't look anything like an agent could be more successful.

Izzy Einstein (on the right in top photo) and Moe Smith teamed to make thousands of arrests.

Early on, Izzy decided he might be more effective with a partner and convinced his friend Moe Smith to leave behind his cigar shop and join him. Almost immediately, Izzy and Moe began to break the mold. They studied the suspected "poison parlors" on their beat and realized they should look like the customers, not cops. In bars that attracted immigrants, Izzy took advantage of his ability to speak German, Polish, and Hungarian, as well as some Italian.

On one of his first assignments, he followed a regular customer into a bar in Brooklyn wearing an old, rumpled suit. The bartender laughed when he ordered a near beer.

Patiently, Izzy explained, he was new to the area and didn't know the customs. But just to prove he was for real, he said he would buy a pint of whiskey, if it wasn't too expensive. The bartender sold him one—and Izzy made his first arrest.

Early on, he realized he needed liquor as evidence to convince a judge of his bust, but it had to be in a bottle, not in his belly. So he and Moe rigged funnels in the pocket of a coat or vest, connected by a tube to a little bottle in the lining. When they bought a drink, they paid the bartender and then lifted the glass toward their lips. While the bartender was making change, the drink was carefully poured into the funnel.

An outgoing man who loved to entertain, Izzy quickly caught the eye of the gaggle of reporters assigned to cover prohibition's enforcement, who were desperate for good stories. Izzy and Moe cooperated, tipping reporters and photographers off to scheduled raids, spinning great tales of their conquests, and frequently landing on the front pages as New York's most famous "hooch hounds." They wore overalls and tuxedos, posed as pickle sellers and housewares peddlers, and once, they dressed up in football gear and smeared their faces with mud to look like buddies in need of an after-game drink. Even when their pictures were on the wall as a reminder, Izzy found a way to convince the servers that he was someone else. "Nobody suspects a fat man," Izzy explained.

Mostly, the pair simply caught the bartenders and bootleggers off guard. One time, Izzy pinned his prohibition-agent's badge to his coat and strolled into a saloon. "Would you like to sell a pint of whiskey to a deserving prohibition agent?" he asked.

The bartender thought he was hilarious. "That's some badge you've got there," he said, after he sold the pint. "Where'dya get it?" In answer to his question, the seller got to visit headquarters—under arrest.

Frequently, the pair started at dawn, knowing that saloon keepers wouldn't expect agents before 9 a.m. Or they visited on Sundays. Once caught, owners and bartenders sometimes fainted, and one or two collapsed from heart attacks. Twice Izzy faced guns, but he never was injured. Once, the gun jammed, and the second time, he swatted it away, saying, "Murdering me won't help your family."

Noting that bootleggers cursed him and booze-haters praised him, the *New York Times* wrote in 1922 that, "Next to Volstead himself, Izzy Einstein represents all that is good or bad, depending upon the point of view, in the matter of prohibition."

For the first few years of prohibition, Prohibition Bureau chiefs supported the pair. But as the mid-1920s approached, attitudes began to change. What was originally a cat-and-mouse game between the good guys and the bad grew less clear and less funny. After initial compliance, more and more people seemed to be ignoring the law. More than 30,000 illegal speakeasies were believed to be operating in New York, more law enforcement officials were caught taking bribes, and Izzy and Moe's method of dressing up and tricking violators and their self-promotion had lost its charm. On Friday, November 13, 1925, they were let go. In their time as agents, they had arrested nearly 5,000 people and seized some five million bottles of liquor valued at more than $15 million.

The reason for their dismissal, according to one official: "The service must be dignified. Izzy and Moe belong on the vaudeville stage."

An agent closes and padlocks an illegal liquor seller, the action that Leroy Ostransky's family feared most.

Luckily for Leroy Ostransky and his parents, Izzy and Moe never found Sharkey's place. There was one close call, however. To lessen his chances of such a pinch, Sharkey kept as little whiskey as possible in the bar at any one time. One of Leroy's jobs was to help bring new bottles over from their apartment across the street when, at his father's insistence, he went to the saloon's back room each day to practice his violin.

One summer afternoon, his mother slipped a bottle of Old Grand-Dad whiskey into his small music bag. Later, she would bring a couple more bottles over herself. Leroy trudged across the street, and finding his father engaged in a long conversation, he took the bottle in his music bag back to his practice room. He struggled through his hour of practice, never realizing that the usual background noise of the bar had gone silent. When he left the back room, though, he saw the scene his father had worried about for many years.

An agent in a business suit was trying to pry open the cabinet doors below the cash register. Another stood between the bar and the outside door, watching.

And now Leroy was standing in the middle of the room, with the bottle in his music bag suddenly weighing far more than he ever dreamed it could.

"What have you got there, kid?" the agent asked.

Dumbstruck, Leroy could hardly answer. His violin case was in one hand; the music bag in the other. "Where?" Leroy replied. He was frozen in place. If the agent simply asked for his bag, his whole family's livelihood could vanish.

The officer looked to his father. "I'm givin' the kid violin lessons," Sharkey told him.

The agent stared at the boy a few more minutes and then told him to move on. Leroy left the saloon, ready to brag to his friends that he alone, "clever, intrepid, cool beyond imagining—had conned two of the shrewdest, most fearsome representatives of the U.S. Federal Government." But realizing that he was being watched, he headed up the street away from his mother and his apartment.

The agents found nothing illegal that day.

When the danger had passed, Leroy returned to the saloon to find his mother and father sitting at the bar waiting for him. They shared their stories: A regular customer had seen the men head toward the saloon, and alerted Sharkey, who quickly dumped all the drinks and sealed a secret compartment under the sink. But his dad had forgotten about the bottle in Leroy's bag until his son finished practicing. "We could've lost the store," his mother told him.

Leroy shared how he had escaped the enemies, and then turned his bag—the bottle still inside—over to his mother. Many years later, as a prominent composer and music professor, he savored his time as an outlaw. "I still relish the moment," he wrote. "I was a valued member of the family; I was, at least for the moment, a partner."

CHAPTER 7
MILK AND MOONSHINE

I N THE SAME Washington office buildings where the notion of national prohibition grew from a pie-in-the-sky idea to a part of the Constitution, illegal liquor, by many accounts, became a regular fixture. In the Capitol restaurant, a waiter accidentally dropped a bottle of whiskey. Someone else dropped one on the first floor of the U.S. House office building. Legislators appeared drunk on the House and Senate floors. Others were caught returning from overseas trips with liquor in their luggage. Then, in one particularly embarrassing moment, two bootleggers got into a slugfest over who had the right to serve white corn liquor to those on the House building's second floor.

A thirsty *Washington Post* reporter once asked his favorite bootlegger for some gin. The bootlegger took him on a short drive around the Treasury building to the hedge of the White House. There, he pulled out a burlap bag and filled his pockets with small bottles, before carefully replacing his stash. His hiding place was never discovered. After all, who would look for a bag of booze on the White House lawn?

New York had its multiplying number of speak-

Children race to scoop up wine that police officials in New York City poured into the streets.

easies and illegal saloons, but Washington had many bootleggers, who built their reputations on their product quality, prices, and reliable delivery. Liquor was available largely to those who could afford it, since even the cheap stuff went for as much as $7 a gallon, or about $87 in today's dollars.

Most members of Congress had voted for the dry law, but, said one reporter, "Capitol Hill was one of the wettest spots in Washington."

Alice Roosevelt Longworth, the daughter of former President Theodore Roosevelt, thought many politicians took the law seriously at the start, but that their conviction didn't last very long. Her husband, U.S. Representative Nicholas Longworth, who would become Speaker of the U.S. House in 1925, opposed saloons.

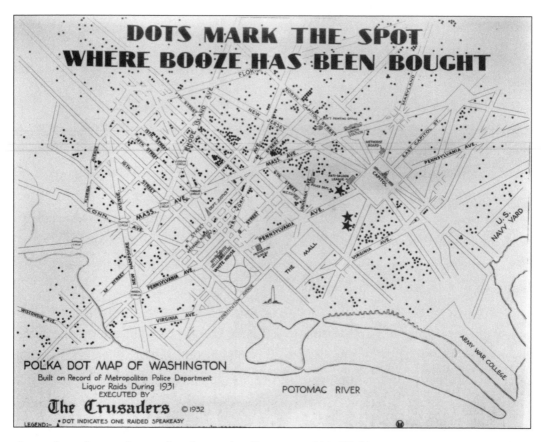

A map shows the stunning number of spots where liquor was sold in Washington.

But he "did not have the slightest intention of complying with the Eighteenth Amendment," she said. Instead, she wrote later, "When it first came in we grumbled, shrugged our shoulders, decided to use the stock we had, and when that was gone turn our attention to wine making and distilling." The butler used oranges and a small still to make "a passable gin," and the family bought pounds of grapes for their own wine. For a time, they also made beer in the cellar, until supply later became so plentiful that home brewing was no longer necessary.

Under Warren Harding, who was elected in 1920, the White House was as wet as the Potomac River. Before unofficial dinners, cocktails were served in the upstairs hall outside the president's quarters. Even during big, official receptions, the upstairs might be open to a different kind of party. One night, during one of those receptions, Longworth went upstairs herself to see if the rumors she had heard were true. There, in a room heavy with tobacco smoke, with President Harding's much-loved playing cards and poker chips at the ready, every brand of whiskey imaginable was on display.

Like the upstairs and the downstairs at the White House, there were really two Americas under prohibition. A large percentage of Americans probably followed the law, either because they believed drinking was wrong, they couldn't afford the illegal stuff, or obeying the law was the right thing to do. Growing up in Washington, the children's book author Jean Craighead George recalled that her parents and their friends simply didn't drink and prohibition simply wasn't an issue. "We were busy doing other things," she says.

Retired Supreme Court Justice John Paul Stevens, who joined the high court in 1975, grew up in Chicago in a family of teetotalers. His parents "always taught us to avoid Demon Rum, that it was bad stuff," he said. He knew there were bootleggers, but didn't know any, and his own neighborhood was law-abiding. Chicago was prospering, he remembered, and "for me, it was a very happy time."

For people who wanted to drink, the tight supply of any kind of beer or liquor created an immediate problem. Quite simply, there wasn't enough to go around, and what was available was often too expensive for the middle class. During the 1920s, milk and soft drinks like Coca-Cola became ready substitutes, and the amounts consumed almost tripled. In many small and mid-sized communities, the social customs largely discouraged drinking.

As with the propaganda battles betweens the wets and the drys in the years

Officials search a group for illegal flasks of whiskey.

leading up to prohibition, the perspective on how prohibition was going depended on the politics of the person you asked. Many government officials argued that a more sober nation was leading to safer streets, less drunkenness, and fewer crimes. A study in Massachusetts found that more students were attending school regularly, fewer teens were in trouble with the law, and fewer children were neglected or abused. Roy Haynes, who as Prohibition Commissioner led the Prohibition Bureau, declared that prohibition was "the most dominating and determining force" in "emptying hospitals, asylums, and jails; rapidly accumulating savings, overflowing schools, sturdier, happier children, better, more prosperous homes, increasing and more wholesome recreation, healthier social life, and increased fruits of human labor."

To that impressive list, one owner added a booming business at beauty salons. "When men drank, they were not so critical," Mrs. Harry Newton Price told the *New York Times*. But now that men were sober and could see the wrinkles and straight hair of their partners, "women are flocking to beauty parlors."

By the mid-1920s, prohibition had become the hottest subject of the day, discussed and written about almost daily. Many people weren't very happy about the situation—as Morris Sheppard learned on a visit to Chicago. The father of national prohibition was sitting in a barber's chair for a shave when the barber began to

Despite prohibition, stores openly advertised cocktail shakers, liquor sets, and silver flasks.

lecture him about his displeasure with the Eighteenth Amendment. As a barber made large strokes across Sheppard's face with his sharp razor, he ranted that "he would like to get his hands on the bird who had 'put over' prohibition on the American people." Sheppard didn't dare offer an opinion—or identify himself. He felt lucky to escape unscathed.

Books about prohibition rolled off the presses, many magazines featured a prohibition story in nearly every issue, and the *New York Times* wrote more than 16,000 stories mentioning it between 1920 and 1927, many of them on the front page. The stories frequently painted a distressing picture, a collage of new developments in home brewing, bootlegging, and speakeasies, especially among immigrants, the wealthy, and the young.

Immigrants, accustomed to wine and beer at mealtimes, simply found a way to make various brews at home rather than stopping at a saloon. The wealthy continued to insist on a regular supply of their favorite drinks, funding an enormous underground economy that smuggled or illegally manufactured huge quantities of the stuff on their behalf.

The young of the 1920s already were making their parents wince with their new habits and styles. Girls and women cut their long hair into short bobs, tossed aside heavy skirts for the skimpy, straight dresses of flappers, and used rouge to color their cheeks, a habit their parents found offensive, if not immoral. Smart, up-and-coming young men carried flasks of whiskey on their hips in defiance of the law, and—most appalling of all—the girls began to drink right along with them, in public, no less. It was a sure sign to many older adults that the next generation was headed for certain ruin.

Young people in particular took to hiding liquor-filled flasks in their jackets, pockets, and even garters.

College students, who had long enjoyed beer or something stronger, hardly missed a beat. Surveys on a number of campuses all through the 1920s showed that more students drank than didn't, and by the middle 1920s, the majority of students on many campuses, including Yale, Princeton, Illinois, and Ohio Western Reserve, favored changing or repealing the law.

Most disturbing, however, was the way the rebellion against the law touched children and teens.

In households where family members were brewing or distilling, children were recruited to help and sometimes to share in the spoils. As a boy living next to his grandparents and aunt and uncle, the writer James A. Maxwell recalled that his grandfather grew increasingly short-tempered after his supply of beer ran out in 1923—until the whole family started brewing together.

Young James won the important job of adding sugar to bottles with a funnel and then passing them to his mother, who used a siphon and a filter to fill them with beer. His father applied the caps. The Monday night family bottling sessions

Many families tried to distill liquor at home, a dangerous undertaking given the temperatures and equipment needed to make spirits.

became a treasured get-together, he remembered, that "provided an opportunity to discuss and dispose of clan problems, and to a small degree, to enjoy the flounting [sic] of a despised law."

Around the perimeter of the nation, young rumrunners found ways to bring foreign liquor to the United States. In upstate New York and in northern Michigan, daring teenagers and young men drove into Canada and packed their cars with beer or whiskey for nighttime trips home.

From Detroit, boats headed to Canada during spring and summer days, often motored by drivers in their teens. There, they loaded up, leaving the Canadian docks before dark, as required. They sat in the water waiting for signals—red, green, or flashing lights—that told them the coast was clear. Then they hurried their precious cargo, sometimes towing barges of crates behind them, into American ports.

Much of it headed to an outpost south of Detroit called Ecorse, where some 500 boats worked the river. When the boats came in during the night hours, workers were ready to unload them straight to trucks, which would then barrel out down the winding roads to Detroit, Ohio, and other places farther south. Boys of thirteen to sixteen acted as lookouts and messengers, watching for police or other trouble, and sometimes handling truck deliveries themselves.

A mere thirty customs agents per shift worked the area to stop the trade, and federal agents sometimes seemed to shoot indiscriminately, with young people caught in the crossfire. In 1925, customs agents shot several bullets at a boat manned by three boys, sons of prominent local businessmen, nearly hitting the occupants.

In May 1927, federal agents rammed a boat carrying James Lee and his eleven-year-old daughter, Mildred, who were out enjoying a day on the river. Both of them were killed, and the federal boat sped off without stopping to provide aid. Local citizens were outraged and protested the government's harsh actions to Washington. But many shrugged and considered it, like poisonous alcohol and the occasional shootout, to be merely part of the enforcement of the Eighteenth Amendment.

With high school boys and girls open to experimenting, speakeasies began to target them, just as the saloons had. More than a dozen operated in Chicago within blocks of three high schools. In Pittsburgh, young boys could fill their flasks at seventeen different places on a single residential street. And in Detroit, residents were both appalled and captivated by the story of Kenneth Nestell, a fourteen-year-old Detroit boy arrested in March 1924 after a drunken rage in which he smashed pictures and furniture at a blind pig that had served him whiskey.

Describing his skin as "dead white," his copper-colored hair "long and scraggly," and his eyes "old and tired-looking," the *Detroit News* reported that Kenneth had been a drunkard for several months, had made it to school only "when he was sober enough," and "had recently been moved back a grade." Kenneth told investigators that three years before, the operator of the blind pig had pushed him to take a drink. "I didn't want the drink but he kept on till I took it," he said. Later, he began to want liquor more often, and would steal for the operator in exchange for whiskey.

The local newspaper jumped on the story of Kenneth Nestell, discovering many blind pigs near local schools.

The "horrifying revelations" led to the discovery that several blind pigs were operating around schools. They weren't necessarily saloons or cabarets—in more than 300 raids over the next few weeks, police confiscated almost 39,000 quarts of liquor from places like cigar stores, laundries, tailors, and barber shops. Candy stores, it turned out, also frequently (and secretly) sold strong drinks as well.

What were Americans drinking if legitimate brewers and distillers were outlawed? There were almost no limits to their creativity and determination in finding ways to make, smuggle, and buy beer, wine, and liquor, even though the results sometimes made them sick, maimed them, or worse, occasionally killed them.

Beer could be hard to come by, except in big cities. Legitimate brewers could make and sell a very weak beer, though, interestingly, they had to make the real stuff first and then remove the alcohol. Not surprisingly, some brewers simply skipped the removal step and shipped the real stuff to customers, prompting Anheuser-Busch to complain that, "those who are obeying the law are being ground to pieces by its very operation, while those who are violating the law are reaping unheard-of rewards. Every rule of justice has been reversed."

Legal sales of liquor required a prescription, and doctors—and sometimes the pharmacists themselves—wrote them for just about any ailment.

Since fermented fruit beverages could be made for personal use, California grape growers expanded their vineyards—almost too much—and shipped carloads of grapes across the country for home winemakers. In grocery and department stores, packages of dehydrated grapes were sold with labels that read something like this: "WARNING! If the contents of this package are added to 5 gallons of water, 5 lbs. of sugar, and 1 cake of yeast, the result will be an intoxicating beverage which is illegal in the United States." A brick of grape concentrate, customers were told, shouldn't be put in a jug, corked, and set in a dark place for three weeks or shaken once a day because—hint, hint—it would turn into wine.

In Washington, D.C., many doctors charged $2 to $3 for a whiskey prescription, with no symptoms, questions, or real names required—though courtesy might call for the patient "to murmur something about a pain in the back of his neck." Druggists could fill the prescriptions with smuggled fare or pints from government warehouses, though as Leroy Ostransky found, they often watered them down and shared the extra with bootleggers and speakeasies.

The worst of the pharmacy concoctions was a nasty potion called Jamaican Ginger, which sold for 30¢ to 50¢ and was mixed with a drink from the drugstore's soda fountain. A few drops were supposed to cure a stomachache, but too much of the two-ounce bottles destroyed nerves and muscles. The symptoms started slowly, with numbness, and before too long, victims couldn't use their index fingers or thumbs, and their feet drooped helplessly from their ankles, thwacking the floor as they walked.

The malady, known as "jake paralysis," could be permanent, and ultimately affected an estimated 15,000 people, mostly in Kansas, Oklahoma, and other parts of the region. Only later did chemists discover that the paralysis was caused by replacing the ginger with a cheaper substitute: chemicals that were so toxic, they were later developed into deadly nerve gases during World War II.

Industrial alcohol was another potential source of drink. Production of pure alcohol for use in foods, medicines, chemicals, and other products tripled during the 1920s, reflecting both a boom in new products and demand for anything alcoholic. A portion of industrial alcohol was allowed to remain pure and was supposed to be taxed and tightly controlled.

Another portion, intended for car antifreeze and paints, was tainted with poisons that could cause blindness or death if drunk. A third portion, for use in goods like perfumes, dyes, and hair tonics, had fewer, less lethal chemicals, some of which could be removed by industrial bootleggers.

A sizeable quantity of that industrial alcohol ended up in the bellies of American drinkers, killing hundreds and then thousands of people a year. In some ways, it was amazing that more people didn't die: Of almost 500,000 gallons of liquor confiscated in New York one year, 98 percent contained some poison.

Anywhere there was alcohol, someone found a way to drink it. In Texas, a grocer admitted that he sold twenty times as much lemon extract as before prohibition and he shared a simple recipe: Chip out a rounded section of a block of ice and pour in the extract. In a few minutes, the now-chilled lemon flavoring becomes gummy, while the alcohol separates and floats on top, a quick drink for 30¢.

Perhaps the biggest supply of all came from homemade moonshine, distilled in kitchens and living rooms and in secluded spaces across rural America in quantities too large to begin to measure. With corn, potatoes, or other grains, some yeast, and a way to heat and cool the mess, just about any daring and enterprising

Alcohol tainted with chemicals or poisons was a huge risk, killing thousands of people during the prohibition years.

moonshiner could set up his own alcohol maker, or "alky cooker." Teachers had complained of children "coming to school under the influence of drink." In tiny Sugar Notch, Pennsylvania, a reverend said he had seen women and children tending stills and drinking their output. When he asked a congregant if he would say that one out of five homes had a still, the answer was blunt: Only one out of five homes *didn't* have one, he was told.

The distilling conditions, whether out of doors or in crowded city homes, were less than clean and sanitary. Prohibition agents sometimes found dead cats, rats, mice, and insects floating in the mucky soup that would be distilled into liquor.

Perhaps the clearest picture of the two roads Americans took under prohibition can be found by following the growing popularity of the automobile in the 1920s. In 1916, about three million cars roamed the nation's limited roadways. Led by the popularity of Henry Ford's durable Model T, the number tripled to nine million in 1921, and over the decade, it would more than double again, to twenty-three million. At the same time, hundreds of thousands of miles of roads were surfaced or paved, connecting towns and cities, people and their habits as never before.

Ford, the founder of Ford Motor Company, was one of the most prominent businessmen of the day—a brilliant, stubborn, and opinionated man. With unusual policies that called for paying workers well and creating mass production methods to build cars faster and more cheaply, Ford and his company produced a stream of Model Ts that dropped in price from $824 at the start to as low as $260 in 1924.

In the 1920s, Henry Ford and his family owned his company outright, and he set all the rules. He determined worker pay and hours, provided his own parts, and set rigid policies. He hated cigarettes, and smoking was banned at his plants. He also hated alcohol and was one of the country's most outspoken drys—a viewpoint he shared in interviews and books and made clear to his workers.

Henry Ford was famous for making cars affordable, but he was also an outspoken dry advocate.

"Brains and initiative are dulled by even the occasional use of alcohol. They are made permanently dull by even the most moderate habitual use, and they vanish altogether in the steady heavy drinker," he insisted.

Drinking by Ford Motor Company employees was banned not just on the job, but at home, too. Even before prohibition, men from the Ford Sociology Department would go door-to-door visiting workers' homes, and those found to have alcohol or to drink might have their pay cut or be dismissed. "More than once I have had to remove men whom I greatly liked and respected and who had been very capable, just because they decided that a very little liquor out of hours would do them good. I have had to remove them or give them long vacations, not because they were drinking but because they lacked the keenness which their jobs required," Ford said. "Brains and booze will not mix."

At one point, Ford even recommended asking the U.S. Army and Navy to enforce the Volstead Act, in effect turning the U.S. military on its own citizens. (The suggestion was ignored.) Yet for all of his efforts, Ford could only do so much to change others' behavior. Blind pigs flourished around his plants in Dearborn, Michigan. And his company's product, the car, was the single greatest contributor to bootlegging, smuggling, and other outlaw behavior.

It was the Model T, in fact, that helped a teenager named Raymond Parks build his own fortune—in moonshine. Raymond was just ten when his mother died, and his father took to drinking heavily. As the oldest of six children in rural Dawson County, Georgia, he took on many of the chores, including driving the family's old Model T to fetch whiskey for his father. One day when he was fourteen, a sheriff's deputy caught him. For some reason, he insisted on telling the judge he was older, which earned him an extended stay in the county jail. "I had gone up the road to get my daddy something to drink, but instead I got three months," he said later. "If I had just told them I was fourteen, I wouldn't have been locked up. I don't know what I was thinking."

In the jail, he met a moonshiner who offered the enterprising young man a way out of the backwoods: a job tending his stills east of Atlanta. A few months after his jail term, Parks left home to learn the basics of whiskey-making, a surprisingly complex process that required soaking, sprouting, and drying corn to turn its starch into sugars; grinding and soaking the corn sugar to turn it into "sweet mash," and then fermenting it into sour mash, changing the sugar to alcohol. Only then was the smelly mess ready to be distilled; this separated the alcohol from the other liquids.

Moonshiners strained the liquid through a bed sheet or cloth and cooked it in big covered kettles. While water turns to steam at 212 degrees Fahrenheit, alcohol turns to vapor at a lower temperature. The trick was to heat the liquid just enough to turn the alcohol to steam, which flowed out a small pipe into a coil, or "worm." The coil was cooled with water, turning the steam inside the pipe back into liquid.

Bootleggers cleverly designed this truck to appear that it was carrying a load of lumber.

But that wasn't the end of it. The first round of distilling left impurities, so the liquid had to be heated and run through the worm at least one more time. Even then, the first and last parts of the batch—the heads and the tails—were poisonous and had to be thrown away. Customers judged the brew by shaking it and looking at the foam, or "bead," that formed at the top. Tight bubbles meant high-proof liquor; loose, collapsing bubbles meant the whiskey was weak.

Raymond coaxed whiskey from the stills for two years, doing well enough to operate his own stills on the side and buy two cars, a used Model T and a snazzier Chevrolet. When he was sixteen, an uncle tracked him down and enticed Raymond to come work at his service station and garage in Atlanta. There, he learned the ins and outs of cars—and another side to the moonshine business. His uncle also paid Raymond handsomely to drive back to the hills and rural areas at night to pick up square gallon tins of corn whiskey and run them back to Atlanta, where his uncle would pour them into pint and quart jars for resale.

"I would head to Dawsonville right after we locked up [and] load sixty gallons in my T-model," he remembered. On the way home, he would stop at a creek to wash the dirt and mud off his tires, "so not to attract attention" and to "blend with the morning traffic to Atlanta."

On the nights when his uncle didn't need him, he made his own runs for up to a hundred gallons, stacked and covered with a blanket in the back where the seats used to be. His side business netted him a profit of 30¢ a gallon, or up to $30 a night, at a time when a prohibition agent might make $10 or $12 a day. Eventually, he decided to hire hands to make moonshine just for him, realizing he could increase his profits.

Parks stands by one of his cars at an early Daytona Beach race.

Still, the work was dangerous and risky. Hauling hundreds of pounds of sloshing liquor down country roads in the dark in a jalopy was hazardous enough. But he also had to contend with the police. One day, an unmarked car passed him on the highway and then pulled in front to cut him off. Moving quickly, Parks slammed on the brakes and tore out of the car across a field, scrambling into a thicket to lose the officer. Over time, he abandoned more than one whiskey-laden car that he would never recover.

By the time he was eighteen, Raymond had made enough money to buy his uncle's service station and a farm, where he moved some brothers and sisters from a family that had grown to sixteen children. He also learned how a creative mechanic could make a car reach unheard-of speeds and how moonshine drivers could calmly navigate the most treacherous roads at stunning speeds. When car racing became a popular weekend sport several years later, he became an early team owner, and later helped found the racing circuit known as NASCAR, originally fueled by daring drivers who grew up running moonshine through the backwoods of the South.

Used in ways that Henry Ford could hardly have imagined, cars like Raymond Parks's Model T carried home-brewed whiskey from rural areas to urban ones all over the country and smuggled liquor across borders. The frequent runs made police in some areas quick to try to stop—or even shoot at—speeding cars. At one point, tensions got so high in Michigan that the attorney general had to ban an early window sticker that read, "Don't Shoot, I'm Not a Bootlegger."

In the big, teeming cities, the cars began to serve another purpose: They became something of a weapon in the hands of big-wheel operators who controlled much of the area's supply of liquor and beer. By the late 1920s, in fact, the phrase "to take for a ride" would acquire a double meaning.

CHAPTER 8
SNORKY AND SCARFACE

"I VIOLATE THE PROHIBITION LAW—sure," Al Capone told a newspaper reporter in 1927, for the whole world to see. "Who doesn't?"

Of course, not everyone violated the prohibition law quite like Al Capone. As the leader of the most powerful gang in Chicago, he oversaw a brewing, bootlegging, and gambling business that brought in what officials estimated as close to $100 million a year (or more than $1 billion a year in today's dollars). And, on more than one occasion, he had—quite literally—gotten away with murder.

Still, Capone saw himself more as a public servant than as one of the nation's most dangerous criminals. "I've been spending the best years of my life as a public benefactor," he told another newspaper. "I've given people the light pleasures, shown them a good time. And all I get is abuse . . ."

"Public service is my motto," he went on. "Ninety-nine percent of the people in Chicago drink and gamble. I've tried to give them decent liquor and square games. But I'm not appreciated."

Before 1920, when alcohol was legal, street gangs in the big cities were little more than a rag-tag

Al Capone, the notorious gangster, operated for years outside the law.

collection of angry young men who specialized in illegal vices, like gambling. But the arrival of the Eighteenth Amendment fueled the rise of aggressive and violent gangsters like yeast in bread.

Making, distributing, and selling beer and liquor was a natural fit for the expertise of a gang like Capone's, as well as gangs in cities like New York, Detroit, Kansas City, Philadelphia, Cincinnati, and St. Louis. To feed the seemingly endless thirst, the chiefs of these underground businesses produced and delivered a plentiful supply of beer and moonshine. To offer the best whiskeys, rums, and brandies to their best customers, they struck deals for regular deliveries from big rumrunners and smugglers around the nation's northern and eastern borders.

There was only one hitch: In a free-for-all, every-man-for-himself enterprise, every gangster wanted a bigger share of the trade. As individual gangsters became more demanding and territorial, few stopped to settle differences with discussion and negotiation. A revolver worked better. And even more effective was a Thompson submachine gun, or Tommy gun, an innovation of the Great War that could fire off hundreds of shots a minute—and more than 1,000, if specially equipped.

By the mid-1920s, few gangsters were more familiar with the Tommy gun than the man they called Scarface, Alphonse Capone.

Born in Brooklyn in 1899, Alphonse was the fourth of nine children. His father, Gabriel, a barber, and his mother, Theresa, had emigrated from Italy just a few years before. Al attended a local elementary school and was a steady "B" student until the sixth grade, when he skipped school more often than he went. After falling behind, he was forced to repeat sixth grade. One day, according to one story, his teacher scolded him and he hit her. After a whipping by the principal, Al quit school for good, though he was barely a teen. Later, he would say he dropped out to help support his growing family.

For a while, he worked at legitimate jobs: as a clerk in a candy store, setting up pins at a bowling alley, and as a paper and cloth cutter at a box company. Within a couple of years of leaving school, he was learning the rules of the streets, running with a tough crowd of young goons-in-training, and getting an education in how to use his fists and shoot a gun. By the time he was eighteen, he had taken another job, at a Coney Island saloon run by an up-and-coming gangster, where Al worked his way up from dishwasher to bartender.

One evening, when a woman shunned his advances, he kept at it, ultimately insulting her loudly enough for others to hear. Her brother demanded an apology. Instead, the bigger Capone came at him. The brother pulled a knife and aimed for Capone's neck. He missed, but slashed Capone's face in three places. It would take thirty stitches to knit up his left cheek, and the purple scar would remain forever. Later, Al would try to pass it off as an injury from World War I—but he had never served in the military.

" 'AT'S THE BABY"

October 17, 1926

The Thompson submachine gun, developed for World War I, became a frightening symbol of 1920s gang warfare.

Before his teens were over, he was a father and husband, and had been arrested three times— once for disorderly conduct and twice for investigation of murder. He had already displayed a knack for cold-blooded brutality. Intending to rob a young man who had just won a wad of cash in a dice game, Capone stuck a gun in the man's stomach. When the man implied he would turn Capone in, Capone pulled the trigger.

The victim, young Capone said, should have known better.

Capone was arrested but, thanks to his gangland friends, never charged or convicted.

Capone's hot head got him in trouble again the next year, when he pummeled a low-level gang member in a barroom fight. Not waiting to find out if the law—or a gun-toting gangster—would find him, he accepted an offer to help out a transplanted Brooklyn gangster who was building quite a business in Chicago.

Capone's timing couldn't have been better. He moved his wife, Mae, and their boy "Sonny" from New York to Chicago in 1919, on the eve of prohibition and just shy of his twenty-first birthday. His first stint was at a nightclub named the Four Deuces for its address, 2222 South Wabash Avenue, where he was a bartender, bodyguard, and chauffeur. He rented the storefront next door and filled it with junk. Then he had business cards printed saying, "Alphonse Capone, second hand furniture dealer," a cover for his less savory activities.

He was reportedly an efficient and violent thug. Capone would drag men with useful information into the Four Deuces cellar and torture them until they spilled the beans. Then they would be murdered, their bodies removed through a tunnel and trap door to a car, and dumped on a country road. A dozen men may have died that way.

Within months, Capone established himself as a reliable lieutenant to his mentor, a gangster named Johnny Torrio, and together they began to build an enormous beer business. With help from out-of-work brew masters, they created an elaborate network of breweries, trucks, and speakeasies, paying off cops, judges, and politicians as they went. Other gangs specialized in alcohol and moonshine, and occasionally sparred for beer customers with Capone and Torrio.

"We figured this law wasn't making the biggest hit in the world with a lot of people," Capone said later. "They didn't vote for it and didn't want it, and was America a free country or what? It looked like a good opening for a lot of smart younger fellows."

By 1923, the Chicago Crime Commission listed Alphonse Capone, also known as Scarface Capone and Al Brown, at the top of a list of twenty-eight so-called public enemies or "persons who are constantly in conflict with the law." But the local news reporters, who often assigned gangsters oddball nicknames like "Greasy Thumb," "Bottles," and "Potatoes," just for fun, hadn't caught on. There, he was often called Al Brown or Al Caponi, and occasionally Alfred.

By then, Capone, a burly man of 5 feet, 10 inches and more than 200 pounds, was starting to mature. After his father died suddenly in 1920, he brought his mother and several of his brothers and sisters to Chicago and moved them into a two-story house. He sent his youngest sister, Mafalda, to a private school, and every Christmas, he loaded up a car with candy, fruit, turkeys, and gifts for teachers and students alike. He became known for pulling out a wad of bills and peeling off generous tips to newsboys, hatcheck girls, and waitresses, and helping the poor buy coal, food, and clothing in the winter. Later, he bought elaborate gifts for friends and those who helped him: $275 diamond belt buckles, combination watches and cigarette lighters, and beaded handbags. As his business and the bulging rolls of cash in his pocket grew, he also grew bolder and more violent.

Capone is surrounded by family and friends at a 1929 picnic.

A Chicago Cubs player autographs a ball for Capone and his son, Sonny, at a charity baseball game.

During a crackdown on bootleggers in Chicago, Capone and Torrio moved their operation to the western suburb of Cicero, a town of 75,000 with an accommodating local government. In the spring of 1924, local Republican officials sought help from the Torrio-Capone men in their reelection. That kind of uneasy cooperation, where gangs helped politicians with elections and politicians helped gangsters with their legal troubles, dated back to the 1840s and allowed both sides to become more powerful.

In Cicero, the Capone crowd turned out in force. The night before the election, Capone men busted into the office of the Democratic candidate for town clerk, beating him and ransacking the place. The next day, a dozen cars loaded with armed thugs cruised the streets, making sure the election went their way. Voters found strangers hovering over them, sometimes using their fists, sometimes yanking the ballots from their hands to make sure the vote went for the Republicans. Democratic workers were kidnapped and held in a hotel basement. At least three men were killed.

Citizens appealed to the county for help, and squads of Chicago policeman and detectives arrived in the late afternoon to try to disperse the roving brutes. Near dusk, police in unmarked cars and civilian clothes pulled up and approached the gang. Shots were fired. Most of the gang members got away, but one of Capone's older brothers, Frank, was hit and killed.

Not surprisingly, the gang-favored politicians won the election—at a price. Capone and Torrio now had free reign for their enterprises. Once, when the town president didn't carry out a Capone order, the gangster went to city hall and demanded that the man follow him outside. There, Capone hit him and knocked him down the city hall stairs. Even elected officials needed to know who was boss.

Some weeks after the election, Capone tracked down a man who had roughed up a friend of his, and he put six bullets in his head—in front of three witnesses. The police, certain that Capone was the murderer, began to search for him. While they looked, the witnesses completely forgot what they had seen.

Days later, Capone appeared at the police station, saying he heard the police were looking for him.

When questioned, Capone denied any knowledge of the shooting. He was merely an antiques dealer, he explained.

"He is guilty," a police officer said, "but we have not enough evidence on which to hold him." Capone walked out as he had walked in.

Not long after, the gangland wars exploded. Dion "Dean" O'Banion, a popular florist by day and bootlegger by night, began to challenge the Torrio-Capone gang's territory. His thugs tried to bully saloon owners to buy their beer from him, and he began paying police more for protection than Capone paid. One day, while O'Banion was clipping chrysanthemums for a big funeral, three men entered the shop. One shook the florist's hand and held on, while another delivered five bullets into his body at close range, and a sixth into his head.

Mourners sent $100,000 worth of flowers to the funeral.

In revenge, Capone's car was raked with bullets—but he wasn't inside. (He did, however, replace his car with a $20,000 armored Cadillac with bullet-proof glass and a gun box in the back.)

Johnny Torrio got it worse. Returning from a shopping trip with his wife, the two were unloading packages when a car drove up and began firing. He was shot three times, but the assassin ran out of bullets before he could deliver the last one to the head. Torrio recovered, but retired from the gangster business, leaving control of the west side of Chicago to 26-year-old Al Capone.

The killings continued and escalated. Dozens of men were shot in 1926 by a passing car or "taken for a ride," lured or forced into a car and then murdered and dumped on a deserted road. Police would show up and investigate, and occasionally make arrests. But with gang members keeping a code of silence, no one ever seemed to be tried and convicted.

Citizens shrugged off much of the killing as fighting among hoodlums—until May 1926, when three men were gunned down in Cicero. Only two were gangsters, it turned out. The other was a popular young assistant state attorney named William McSwiggin.

What McSwiggin was doing with the two thugs wasn't known, but this much was: His shooting was unacceptable, an outrage. The murder of a public official made national headlines, and suddenly, all eyes were on Al Capone.

After disappearing for a time, Capone went on the offensive. He reappeared at the police station, saying, "I understand I'm wanted for the McSwiggin killing. I know nothing about it." He contacted reporters and granted interviews. Ultimately, investigators couldn't find enough evidence to even charge him with the crime, and he went back to his business as something of a hero and celebrity, a man so clever and powerful that he was truly above the law.

Young prosecuting attorney William McSwiggin is laid to rest after he was shot down. Capone was the chief suspect.

While the police couldn't seem to pin him down, Capone was regularly available to reporters. Once, when a reporter knocked at his house, Capone came to the door wearing a pink apron and bedroom slippers and carrying a pan of spaghetti. He granted a short interview and then, presumably, returned to eat dinner. Another time, he gave an interview just three hours after a Chicago gang boss and his bodyguards were riddled with bullets. Patricia Dougherty, a reporter for the *Chicago Herald and Examiner*, noted that Capone was just twenty-seven years old, but looked at least forty. That day, she found herself in the odd position of delivering a message from him via the newspaper.

"I told him I wanted peace and he wouldn't take it. Instead he came out here and shot up the town—and today he got killed," Capone said of the recently departed man. "Now if any of his mob that's left wants to make peace with me, I'm ready. Tell them that, will you?"

"I told them," Dougherty wrote later, "In the strangest interview I ever wrote, I told the North Side crowd Capone was giving them their last chance. That he didn't want to die. That he believed there was enough beer business for all of them."

Still, she remained shocked by all the violence she had seen and written about, the more than a hundred men who had been murdered in two years, and how the

With his characteristic cigar, Capone relaxes at his second home in Miami, Florida, in 1930.

police seemed "powerless and useless" in the face of so much terror and graft. "It is a story so fantastic, so bizarre and un-American that even as I write it I wonder if I've really seen all the things that I know to be true," she said in 1927.

In interviews, Capone showed a reflective and sentimental side that seemed inconsistent with a man so casual about vicious behavior. He was so self-conscious about his scar that he was said to powder his face to tone it down and he frequently turned his left cheek away from news cameras so it wouldn't show.

He complained to reporters that he didn't like being called "Scarface." When that didn't stop the name-calling, he made appointments with their editors and pleaded his case with them. It didn't help, of course, but he kept trying. Among friends, he preferred to be called "Snorky," 1920s slang for elegant or stylish.

He had high aspirations for his son. "What do I want my boy, Albert, to be when he grows up? Well, first of all, I want him to be a man. A brave man who can look anyone in the eye and stand his ground no matter what comes. I like a man with nerve—even if he's [at] the other end of a gunfight.

"I want him to have all the things I never had. I want him to go to college. I went to work when I was thirteen. I want him to know about nice things in the world. I don't want him to be a bootlegger or a reformer, either. I'd rather like him to be a professional man, a doctor, a lawyer, or a businessman. Anything that'd give him an easier time than his old man's had.

"What do I want him to think about me? I want him to know that I loved him enough to risk my life to work for him. I want him to remember that I had a different kind of a life than I made for him and I expect him to repay me by playing the game straight. And most of all, what I want for that boy is a wife like mine and boy like mine to make whatever game he picks out worth winning."

Capone didn't admit to any killings, but in that same interview with Dougherty, he explained his view of why they happened: "What does a man think about when he's killing another man in a gang war?" he said. "Well, maybe he thinks that the law of self-defense, the way God looks at it, is a little broader than the law books have it. Maybe it means killing a man who'd kill you if he saw you first. Maybe it means killing a man in defense of your business, the way you make your money to take care of your wife and child. I think it does. You can't blame me for thinking there's worse fellows in the world than me."

He was also frank about who those "worse fellows" were. "There's one thing worse than a crook, I think," he said, "and that is a crooked man in a big political job. A man who pretends he is enforcing the law and is really making dough out of breaking it. Even a self-respecting hoodlum hasn't any use for that kind of fella—he buys them like he'd buy any other article necessary to his trade. But he hates them in his heart."

If so, there was plenty of hate to go around. Capone and his men spent perhaps $15 million a year to line the pockets of and win favors from the police, prohibition agents, and politicians who were supposed to shut him down. Many local officials in and out of Chicago had long ago stopped trying to enforce prohibition laws, leaving the job to federal agents, of whom there weren't nearly enough. Nearly every speakeasy and night club in Chicago and elsewhere paid police to look the other way.

But they weren't the only ones on the take: Politicians protected the gangs in exchange for political donations and support in tough elections. Judges could be bought, too, and if that wasn't enough, juries were often reluctant to convict someone of bootlegging when they might be drinking themselves. One Chicago detective even admitted that some cops would rather kill gangsters themselves—and the police killed a number of them—than watch them be acquitted by a jury.

Prohibition agents were in a category by themselves. Many had a hard time turning away thousands of dollars. During the 1920s, roughly one of every eleven prohibition agents was fired for bribery, extortion, theft, or other violations.

Others, of course, were more dedicated. In Homer, Nebraska, Richard James "Two Gun" Hart earned his nickname for the two pearl-handled pistols he carried at his sides and his sharp gun-handling skills. He worked for a time as a state agent in Nebraska and federal agent in Idaho, North Dakota, and South Dakota, seeking out and shutting down illegal stills. Some days, he made as many as seven raids. He also was charged with manslaughter, but not convicted, for shooting an alleged bootlegger.

Richard "Two-Gun" Hart, Capone's oldest brother and a one-time federal agent, stands by stills he confiscated in North Dakota in the early 1920s.

"Two Gun" had an unusual history. Born in Brooklyn, his given name was Vincenzo "James" Capone—Al's older brother, the oldest Capone child. He ran away at sixteen and took the name of an actor he admired. Just as there were two Americas under prohibition, the wet and the dry, there were also two Capones— the famous gangster and the one-time lawman. Both of them were very good with guns.

Ultimately, it was the big guns and the cold-blooded shooting on February 14, 1929, that turned the brightest lights on Al Capone, leading to his downfall—and maybe beginning the end of prohibition. Capone wasn't in the Cadillac full of men that pulled up to the warehouse garage on Clark Street that Valentine's Day. When the two men in police uniforms and the men in plain clothes entered the warehouse where Bugs Moran's men were waiting, Capone was in Florida. (Ironically, he was at Miami's Dade County courthouse that day talking with district attorneys.)

But the brutality of the murders seemed to bear his mark. The seven unsuspecting Moran men were defenseless, with their backs turned and their hands in the air when the shots flew at them. Some of the slugs ripped across their backs, necks, and heads, and others hit their torsos. Four men fell straight back. Some were so bullet-ridden that their bodies hardly held together.

After the shooting, the men in plainclothes walked out of the garage first, with their hands up, and the men in police uniforms followed, aiming guns at their backs. They all climbed back into the Cadillac, with its police gong and siren, and drove off.

A neighbor who had heard the drumbeat of the guns went to check on the garage and found the grisly sight: six men dead, small rivers of blood running along the floor, the smell of gunpowder hanging in the air. A dog, still leashed to the truck, howled.

Even Chicago police, who had investigated so many gangland murders, had

Police officials re-enact how they believe gangsters carried out the St. Valentine's Day murders.

never seen as gruesome a scene as this. One man was still alive, despite 14 bullets, but he wouldn't say who shot him. He died later that day.

The shocking headlines and gory pictures rocked Chicago and the nation. "Chicago gangsters graduated yesterday from murder to massacre," the *Chicago Herald and Examiner* said, and others concluded that the violence and bloodshed had finally gone way too far. What became known as the St. Valentine's Day Massacre would later make for thrilling movies and fill the pages of crime magazines. But it was an unacceptable reality for everyday America.

As always with gang murders, there were few clues. Police investigated numerous leads, but none of them seemed to go anywhere. Ultimately, fingers pointed at Capone, though there was never enough evidence to back that up. In fact, new research indicates he may not have been involved at all. But at the time, he was the prime suspect, and he quickly became America's Public Enemy No. 1.

A nation's thirst for beer and booze may have made Al Capone and his gang stunningly rich and powerful, but ordinary citizens could no longer ignore the violence and slaughter. That otherwise honest people were snubbing the law was bad enough. But now America seemed to be on the brink of genuine lawlessness. Its most notorious gangster had to be stopped, even if it took the president of the United States to do it.

CHAPTER 9
WET, AGAIN

O N MARCH 4, 1929, less than three weeks after the St. Valentine's Day Massacre, Herbert Hoover was sworn in as America's thirty-first president. With the grotesque scene in Chicago still fresh in the public's mind, he let the rain-drenched crowd gathered for his inauguration know that prohibition and crime were weighing on him.

One of the greatest dangers facing the country "is disregard and disobedience of the law," Hoover said in his inaugural address. The businessman and former Commerce Secretary blamed local and state officials for failing to do their duties but also noted that "a large responsibility rests directly upon our citizens," who, by continuing to drink, were supporting and even encouraging crime.

In a way, he said, the future of America was on the line. "Our whole system of self-government will crumble either if officials elect what laws they will enforce or citizens elect what laws they will support," he warned. "If citizens do not like a law, their duty as honest men and women is to discourage its violation; their right is openly to work for repeal."

Labor union members march for a relaxation of prohibition laws.

Herbert Hoover is sworn in as the thirty-first president, inheriting the problems of prohibition and of gangsters like Al Capone.

He proposed creating a national commission to study crime and law enforcement, including the many abuses under prohibition.

Within months, the commission began its work under the direction of George Wickersham, a former U.S. attorney general. At almost the same time, groups of wealthy and influential citizens ramped up their efforts to repeal the Eighteenth Amendment.

Discussions about repeal, or simply removing the amendment from the Constitution, had begun almost as early as the day the law took effect, but they didn't gain much traction. The Association Against the Prohibition Amendment was formed in late 1920, but it seemed too farfetched to win much credibility. Those opposed to prohibition were more likely to argue for changes to the Volstead Act, such as allowing the sale of some beer and wine.

In 1922, a *Literary Digest* poll of more than 900,000 people found that just under 40 percent approved of the law as it was, a little more than 40 percent favored some changes, and about 20 percent wanted it repealed. But for most of the decade, Congress was still controlled by drys, who had no interest in allowing America to go "moist."

In 1928, the law became part of presidential politics, splitting for the first time along clear party lines. The Democratic nominee, New York Governor Alfred E. Smith, was a Catholic and a dedicated wet who campaigned that the law should be modified or the amendment changed. Opponents dubbed him "Alcohol Al."

On the Republican ticket, Hoover had the support of the drys. He believed in enforcing the Eighteenth Amendment, which he called "a great social and economic experiment, noble in motive and far-reaching in purpose." (Later, he would frequently be misquoted as having called prohibition "the noble experiment," a term he believed could be interpreted in a sneering way.)

Hoover won handily with support from the traditionally Democratic South and the West, a shift many observers attributed more to lingering bigotry and biases against Catholics than a statement about prohibition.

As Hoover was moving toward the presidency, the Association Against the Prohibition Amendment was regrouping. Some of America's wealthiest and most powerful men—including Pierre Du Pont, the retired chairman of both the Du Pont Company and General Motors; ex-senator James Wadsworth, and Charles H. Sabin, president of a New York bank—were frustrated by a law that they believed was eroding respect for government. They wanted states, not the federal government, to determine whether their citizens could drink, and they were stepping up with money and leadership.

Adopting some of the same tactics that the Anti-Saloon League had used fifteen years earlier, they turned up the printing presses, putting out more than a million copies of pamphlets that spelled out prohibition's failures and made news headlines: "Scandals of Prohibition Enforcement" detailed the fierce gang violence, official corruption in more than twenty cities, and the flow of illegal alcohol; "Cost of Prohibition and Your Income Tax" argued that the cost of enforcement plus the lost tax revenue that might be gained from legal liquor was more than all the money the federal government received from individual income taxes; and "Reforming America with a Shotgun: A Study of Prohibition Killings" estimated that 1,000 officers and civilians had lost their lives as prohibition was enforced, far more than the few hundred the government had claimed.

Pauline Morton Sabin helped lead a women's movement whose call for repeal sounded a lot like the WCTU's campaign many years before.

Around the same time, Pauline Morton Sabin, the politically connected wife of banker Charles Sabin, was forming another group, which—like the Woman's Christian Temperance Union decades before—was acting out of concern for America's children. In a 1928 article titled "I Change My Mind on Prohibition," she explained that she once favored the law, hoping young people would never be tempted by drink. But, she wrote, "I am now convinced that it has been proved a failure" and that "children are growing up with a total lack of respect for the Constitution and for the law."

At a Congressional hearing, she heard the WCTU's leader declare, "I represent the women of America."

"Well, lady," Sabin said to herself. "Here's one woman you don't represent."

Though Sabin was on the Republican National Committee and campaigned for Hoover, she decided to form the Women's Organization for National Prohibition Reform in May 1929. Starting with just a few members but drawing on the same kind of well-spoken, passionate, and energetic women who had made the early WCTU so influential, the group made the case that repeal was the only way to protect their children from the evils brought on by the Eighteenth Amendment.

Sabin noted that many mothers of the day were too young to remember saloons, "but they are working for repeal because they don't want their babies to grow up in the hip-flask, speakeasy atmosphere that has polluted their own youth."

Many drys had assumed they would always have the support of women and mothers, but within a year, Sabin's group claimed 100,000 members; within two years, it claimed 300,000.

As the bigger groups organized, others joined the chorus. Labor unions, which had called for changes to the law, now demanded repeal. The American Bar Association, representing the nation's lawyers, adopted a repeal resolution in 1930. In early 1930, *Literary Digest* conducted another poll that highlighted how much opinions had changed: Out of 4.8 million people who responded, just over 30 percent supported prohibition. Just under 30 percent wanted a change to the law. And more than 40 percent—twice the percentage as in 1922—favored outright repeal. The magazine showed the state-by-state breakdown, and most surprising of all, citizens in more than thirty-six states appeared ready to approve it. In other words, if Congress were to let them, the states might very well pass a repeal law.

Morris Sheppard, the author of the original constitutional amendment and the father of national prohibition, was disbelieving. Every year on the January 16 anniversary of prohibition, he made a speech in the U.S. Senate about the value and virtues of the law. In 1930, he told the convention of the Texas Democratic Party that Americans were lucky to have been freed from the liquor interests.

Then he added with confidence, "I want to say to you now that there is as much chance for repeal of the Eighteenth Amendment as there is for a humming bird to fly to the planet Mars with the Washington Monument tied to its tail."

Fifteen years before, when drys filled the state legislatures and Congress with supporters, the wets had been disorganized and disbelieving. This time, the wets were organized and the drys were skeptical and unprepared. Much of the dry organization and financial support had moved on after prohibition was adopted, and those advocates who were left dug in and refused to bend to any kind of compromise.

But problems with prohibition continued to grow, for Hoover and the country.

Posters supporting an end to prohibition promoted the protection of children, much like early posters calling for prohibition.

In 1929 a new law had stiffened the penalties for first-time violators to up to five years in prison and a fine of up to $10,000, from a more modest six months in jail and a $1,000 fine. Those tougher penalties, coupled with stepped-up enforcement, filled the federal prisons to "perilous" levels. In 1930, an Atlanta federal prison built for 2,000 had almost 4,000 inmates, and more on the way. Barracks in Leavenworth, Kansas, and War Department campsites now were holding prisoners as well. And another 13,600 federal prisoners, most of them prohibition violators, were being held in state and county jails.

While the jails were filling and the president was focusing on enforcing laws and stamping out crime, the economy was wobbling. After several years of prosperity, the stock market had rocketed upward in 1928, luring in all kinds of small

Women, children, and a few men rally for repeal of the Eighteenth Amendment in front of the Lincoln Memorial in 1933.

investors, many of whom had borrowed money to buy stocks. The gains had continued into 1929, creating something of a frenzy as even more investors saw stocks as a sure way to riches. But in the summer, the economy began to slow. Car sales, steel production, and home building all dropped off, signaling a business downturn. The nation's banks and financial companies were lending haphazardly, especially to support the stock market craze.

In September, the stock market peaked at an all-time high—and then it began to fall. In October, the plunge accelerated, and over six dark days, ending on Black Tuesday, October 29, more than $25 billion in stock market wealth was

Capone was rarely arrested, but his luck began to run out in 1931.

lost. People who had borrowed money to buy shares in American businesses saw their stocks sold to repay the debt, wiping out their savings.

The stock market hit a bottom in November 1929, and then seemed to recover, regaining almost half its losses by the spring of 1930. But the upturn was temporary, and it soon headed down again, sharply. More and more banks closed. Companies began to let employees go, and as people spent less, more people lost their jobs. The nation's economy was in a steep slide along with the stock market, and nothing Hoover tried to do seemed to help.

Then there was the Capone problem. The gangster now was as internationally famous as the aviator Charles Lindbergh, baseball great Babe Ruth, and

Henry Ford, but for all the wrong reasons. Just after Hoover's inauguration, a group of prominent Chicago men visited Washington to spell out Chicago's dire situation. The city couldn't escape the grip of gangsters and restore order, they said, without help from the federal government. Hoover, realizing it was in his interest to stop Capone as well, directed government agencies to concentrate on Capone.

A team of honest and determined prohibition agents would try to crack down on Capone's brewing business. Meanwhile, another small team of accountants would follow the money, building a case that the notorious and violent gangster had committed the worst of government crimes: He had failed to pay income taxes.

The government got a break when Capone was arrested in Philadelphia in May 1929 for carrying a concealed weapon. Almost overnight, he was sentenced to jail, giving the federal agents some time to build their cases. When Capone was freed after ten months, they had a head start. But it was a tough job: Cleverly, Capone paid cash for everything and didn't even have a bank account, making his money almost impossible to trace.

In June 1931, Capone was indicted for failing to pay income taxes and then for prohibition violations. The tax charges stuck. After a highly publicized trial, in which the government detailed his spending on silk underwear, custom-made suits, church donations, landscaping, and parties, Capone, now thirty-two years old, was convicted and sentenced to eleven years in prison.

In his memoirs, Hoover noted that "it was ironic that a man guilty of inciting hundreds of murders . . . had to be punished merely for failure to pay taxes." *Pathetic* may have been a better word.

As the government was preparing its Capone case, the Commission on Law Enforcement and Observance, also known as the Wickersham Commission, was studying the crime problem. Its final report, in early 1931, outlined in fine detail a failed system rife with crime, corruption, and missed opportunities. But the commission itself concluded that the law shouldn't be changed and the Eighteenth Amendment shouldn't be repealed, leading some people to feel that the whole study was a charade.

The mixed message prompted a *New York World* writer to sum it up in verse:

> *Prohibition is an awful flop.*
> *We like it.*
> *It can't stop what it's meant to stop.*
> *We like it.*
> *It's left a trail of graft and slime,*
> *It don't prohibit worth a dime,*
> *It's filled our land with vice and crime,*
> *Nevertheless, we're for it.*

In 1932, however, a hummingbird apparently prepared to fly to Mars, led more than anything else by the economic woes of the Great Depression. Factories were closing, more banks were failing, and the number of unemployed workers was soaring. Homelessness and hunger were growing common. Supporters of repeal argued that restoring the beer and liquor business would create jobs and new industry, and taxes on beverages and bottles would help a nation desperately in need of income. Bootleggers and speakeasies might have protested, but the times were so miserable that their businesses weren't doing well, either.

The tide was turning. That year, John D. Rockefeller Jr., one of America's richest men and a longtime financial supporter of the drys, stunningly switched sides and called for repeal just before the Republican convention. At that convention, delegates couldn't agree on a prohibition position and adopted a platform that waffled on changing the law. Despite the nation's severe economic troubles, Hoover was nominated again.

In Chicago, the Democratic delegates were much more in agreement. When the party's platform was read aloud, the line "We favor the repeal of the Eighteenth Amendment" stopped the show. The crowd broke into spontaneous yells and cheers, followed by more than ten minutes of dancing, celebrating, and parading around the hall.

Though their candidate, Franklin D. Roosevelt, had wavered on the

Franklin Delano Roosevelt signs a bill to make beer legal again just days after his inauguration in 1933.

prohibition issue in the past, his position was clear now. "This convention wants repeal; this candidate wants repeal, the people of the United States want the Eighteenth Amendment repealed," he declared, to loud applause. "From this date on, the Eighteenth Amendment is doomed!"

Roosevelt, offering new ideas to address the deep and painful economic problems and an end to prohibition, easily won the White House in November. A raft of repeal supporters were elected to the House and the Senate along with him.

In February 1933, before Roosevelt was even sworn in, the Senate took up the repeal question. To try to stop the vote, Morris Sheppard led his own solitary—and unsuccessful—filibuster. The little man stood alone on the floor from 1:30 p.m. until 10 p.m., reading from old documents and reciting columns of figures. But it didn't do any good. The next day, the bill came to the floor and after two days of debate, it passed.

Four days later, the proposal for a new constitutional amendment repealing the Eighteenth Amendment passed the House with the required two-thirds majority. It would be the Twenty-first Amendment, following the Nineteenth, which had given women the vote in 1920, and the just-approved Twentieth, which moved the next president's inauguration to January 20 from March 4.

The first part of the newest amendment was as simple as it could be: "The eighteenth article of amendment to the Constitution of the United States is hereby repealed." The second part protected states that wanted to stay dry by making it illegal to transport liquor across their borders.

Now, at least thirty-six states had to approve the amendment within seven years—with a new twist. The Eighteenth Amendment had been approved by state legislatures that had been packed with the Anti-Saloon League's dry representatives. Under a plan devised by the anti-prohibition groups, voters would elect delegates to state conventions who would then vote on this single issue, bypassing politicians. The method was allowed in the Constitution, but hadn't been used since the Constitution itself was approved.

While the states were organizing their conventions, the new president served up some interim relief. On March 13, nine days after taking office, Roosevelt asked Congress to make beer with 3.2 percent alcohol legal under the Volstead Act. Congress agreed, and on April 7, 1933, hotels, restaurants, clubs, and stores sold the first legal beer in more than thirteen years. More than one million barrels were sold in the first twenty-four hours as happy Americans enjoyed a freedom of choice.

In the same week, Michigan became the first state to approve the Twenty-first Amendment. Several other states followed quickly, including Wisconsin, New Jersey, New York, and Illinois.

The Texas vote was scheduled for August, and Morris Sheppard did his best to make it one of the thirteen states needed to block the amendment. In July, he left Washington in a truck specially equipped with loudspeakers to stump his home state. He traveled 5,000 miles, addressing thousands of people at forty-eight different stops, charging that the repeal effort was led by "millionaires and brewer-ies," and that voters had to stop it.

"Old John Barleycorn is sitting up in his coffin hoping to come alive," he told a group in Hico, Texas, "but he will sit back down if Texas, on Aug. 26, will vote to drive the first of the thirteen nails needed to keep him in his coffin."

Despite Sheppard's persistence and commitment, Texans disagreed with him, overwhelmingly.

The Eighteenth Amendment, voted on during a frightening and costly Great War, had won approval in a mere thirteen months. Now, in the midst of a Great Depression, its demise was even quicker. On December 5, Pennsylvania ratified the amendment just before 1 p.m. Eastern time, sending its decision to Washington by telegraph, motorcycle, and airplane. Ohio followed two hours later. Utah, the thirty-sixth state, had planned to take a long recess that afternoon and vote in the evening, too late for a celebration on the

Old Man Prohibition is hung in effigy as prohibition is finally repealed.

East Coast. But delegates decided they "owed it to the rest of the country" to vote more quickly, and they voted their approval just after 5:30 Eastern time. Bar-tenders, retailers, and government officials sat pinned to radios—which hadn't even existed in 1920—waiting for the news, which was immediately sent by tele-graph to President Roosevelt and the State Department.

In Washington, William Phillips, the acting secretary of state, had already read the proclamation repealing the Eighteenth Amendment a couple of times for photographers and movie cameras. At 5:49:30 p.m., he signed the statement,

A huge crowd gathers at the Hotel Astor in December 1933 to enjoy the first legal liquor in nearly fourteen years.

making it official. The *New York Times* reported that he used a plain pen "that might have been bought for 5 cents anywhere," but that was likely to end up with other important artifacts in the Library of Congress.

An hour later, President Roosevelt, who had been swimming in the White House pool, signed a proclamation calling on citizens "to cooperate with the government in its endeavor to restore greater respect for law and order." White House officials refused to comment on reports that the president had signed the document while still in his swim trunks, a move that might have given new meaning to the term "wet."

In New York, the retail stores Gimbel's and Bloomingdale's opened their wine and liquor departments as soon as the news came over the radio. The lights in Times Square flickered, "Prohibition is dead!" In celebration, "Old Man Prohibition" was hung in effigy, suffered a mock electrocution, and was drowned in a swimming pool. Hotels and restaurants that had obtained permits began serving customers, but only the Hotel Astor had a big crowd.

While eighteen states had approved liquor sales, residents in the other thirty could only wait, some for a few more days, some for months, and some for many years, before they could legally buy a drink again.

For the first—and only—time in American history, a part of the U.S. Constitution had been erased. Americans for decades had wrestled with how to protect their young people from the liquor problem, until a group of organized and determined reformers finally helped push through the most radical and ambitious social experiment ever tried. But instead of a more moral nation, citizens had tasted hypocrisy, drunk bad liquor, witnessed senseless violence, and watched their children ignore the highest law of the land. Now, after thirteen years, ten months, and nineteen days, that era was over.

EPILOGUE
SUCCESS OR FAILURE?

MORRIS SHEPPARD never gave up. Even after prohibition was repealed, he continued to make his anniversary speech every January. For many years, he introduced a new prohibition bill, certain that Americans would come to their senses.

Still, he could chuckle at how things had turned out. For years, he had predicted in his speeches that money that was used to buy clothes or shoes would go to alcohol if it became legal again. Not long after repeal, he was walking down the street and passed a just-opened liquor store. The shop was so new that the old business name was still on the window: One side of the window said "Liquor" in big letters, and the other said, "Shoes."

"From shoes to booze, just as I had said," he told a reporter.

In 1940, he celebrated the twentieth anniversary of prohibition's approval by once more calling repeal a mistake. "We cannot continue to pour nearly two billion gallons of alcoholic poison every year into the veins of our democracy and expect it to survive," he said.

Morris Sheppard died in 1941 at the age of sixty-five, after serving thirty-eight years in Congress. He

Mr. Dry, a prohibition character created by cartoonist Rollin Kirby, oversees the end of an unusual era.

had become an expert on military issues and, in his last year in office, he had helped restart the military draft to help America protect itself as another world war heated up overseas. (Sheppard Air Force Base in Wichita Falls, Texas, would be named after him.) He had rarely missed a day of work, prompting the *Washington Post* to say, "It may be truly said, with deep regret, that he has literally worked himself to death in service to his country."

Al Capone, however, never had a comeback. In May 1932, at the age of thirty-three, he was sent to a federal prison in Atlanta and then transferred to the new isolated federal prison at Alcatraz in 1934. In 1939, with time off for good behavior and suffering from the effects of advanced syphilis, he was paroled and turned over to his family.

Penicillin wouldn't be available for a few more years, and the disease had gone too far for a cure. Treatments helped Capone lead a fairly normal life in Florida for a while, but by 1946, he was, in a friend's words, "nutty as a cuckoo."

On Monday, January 20, 1947, Andrew Volstead, the U.S. representative who had championed the strict rules for prohibition enforcement, died at the age of eighty-six. The next day, Capone suffered a stroke. On January 25, at the age of forty-eight, the man once considered Public Enemy No. 1 died surrounded by his family.

The men who helped launch the prohibition era and the one who filled it with machine-gun fire left a complex legacy. On the surface, an amendment that was passed and then repealed must have been a colossal failure, an embarrassing splotch in America's history.

But prohibition, short-lived though it was, was actually successful in some significant ways. The number of arrests for drunkenness and alcohol-related diseases, like cirrhosis of the liver, fell dramatically. The total consumption of alcohol slid to the lowest level in the nation's history, especially during World War I and the first few years under the Eighteenth Amendment. Although drinking crept back up in the later 1920s and early 1930s, the amount of alcohol consumed per person each year actually remained fairly low for decades, and didn't return to pre-prohibition levels until the 1970s, more than fifty years after prohibition took effect.

In the course of nearly fourteen years of actual prohibition, aided by technology and other developments, Americans became more educated, more urban, and enjoyed far more entertainment. Radios and radio programs became widely available, and almost half the nation became avid listeners. Movie theater attendance doubled after films began to talk in 1926. With one car for every five people, more families headed for national forests and parks. The number of golf courses increased sevenfold. Saloons, the dirty and dangerous blight on the urban landscape, all but disappeared. Even young people had better things to do than to hang out in a bar.

There were political lessons in the battles, too—like the price that both sides paid by refusing to compromise. When the Anti-Saloon League and other dry groups took aim at saloons, the brewers and distillers refused to make changes until prohibition laws were steamrolling their way to the Constitution. But had they responded to the outcry by cleaning up the saloons, or even shutting down the worst ones, the whole prohibition experiment might have been skipped.

The pattern repeated in the late 1920s, when so many Americans told both pollsters and politicians that they wanted just a little beer and wine—and the drys refused to budge. Some believe the Eighteenth Amendment might still be in place today if the drys had agreed to slightly loosen the law.

The experience also drove home the challenge of passing laws that affect an entire country's behavior, especially in a nation as diverse as the United States. "The Twenty-first Amendment taught us that you don't have to have a national rule. States can work things out in different ways," said former Supreme Court Justice John Paul Stevens, who referred to the influences of prohibition at least a couple of times in court opinions before retiring in 2010. "There's always a danger about a national rule that has no exception to it," he said.

In fact, after repeal, states responded in different ways. Oklahoma retained its own prohibition law until 1959, and Mississippi was dry until 1966. Some state governments still run their state's liquor stores to keep others from profiting from booze. Some banned the purchase of mixed drinks for years, requiring diners to bring their own bottles to restaurants. In some places, one voting precinct may be wet while the one next to it is dry.

Even with drinking laws resolved, many of the problems inflamed by prohibition remained. Gangs were so entrenched in gambling operations, protection rackets, and labor unions that removing Capone didn't stop the corruption or end the violence, though worries about crime took a backseat to the bigger problems of the Great Depression. In rural areas, moonshiners continued to make their homemade brew to avoid paying large liquor taxes. The drivers who outran the "revenuers," or tax men, in the 1930s became some of car-racing's earliest champions.

Oklahoma teens protest repeal of the state's prohibitions laws, which voters finally removed in 1959.

Where prohibition failed most, perhaps, was on a more personal level. Alcoholism and alcohol abuse remain significant social problems, affecting more than 17 million American adults and their families. Today's problem of persistent homelessness, often linked to substance abuse and mental illnesses, has the same roots as the problem of drunkenness in the nineteenth century. Parents still worry about protecting their children, especially when government statistics show that an estimated 5,000 young people under the age of twenty-one die each year from alcohol-related car crashes or injuries.

For many years after prohibition ended, however, lawmakers were reluctant to step in too aggressively. In 1980, a group of mothers who lost their children in drunk-driving accidents changed that post-prohibition, look-the-other-way attitude toward drinking and driving. Calling themselves Mothers Against Drunk

Driving, MADD mothers lobbied and created powerful advertising campaigns, listing the names and faces of children who died too young. Their work led to far tougher penalties for drunk drivers and helped raise the legal drinking age to twenty-one from eighteen. Those changes, along with seat belt laws and safer cars, have cut the deaths from drunk driving in half since 1980.

Candy Lightner founded Mothers Against Drunk Driving in 1980 after her daughter Cari was killed by a drunk driver.

School drug and alcohol awareness programs still try to teach children as young as five about the dangers of alcohol and drugs. Many schools participate each October in Red Ribbon Week, encouraging students to pledge to be drug- and alcohol-free. The week was created in the memory of Enrique "Kiki" Camarena, an American drug enforcement agent who was brutally murdered while trying to stop the flow of drugs from Mexico into the United States. The red ribbons his friends and family wore came to symbolize outrage at the damage and pain caused by drug and alcohol abuse.

Today, each of us is accountable for our own behavior, and adult drinking is a matter of choice and personal responsibility. The days of outright prohibition are gone and likely will never return. But the powerful experience of prohibition continues to color our laws, our debates, and our personal lives. And the problems that brought us the Eighteenth Amendment—the pain that substance abuse inflicts on families, the devastation of alcoholism, and the impact of drinking on young people—remain a challenge to current and future generations.

A PROHIBITION AND TEMPERANCE GLOSSARY

THE TEMPERANCE and prohibition movements spawned a rich vocabulary, some of which remains in use today. Here are some of the popular words and their origins.

blind tiger or blind pig An illegal drinking spot, often a low-end bar or a business set up in someone's house or store. Dates back to temperance days and may have come from blinds covering the windows to hide the activity inside or from the blind drunkenness inside. Another theory: because selling liquor was illegal, the "blind pigger" might have offered a look at a "blind pig" for a dime—and given away a free drink with it.

bootlegger A smuggler of illegal alcohol. Believed to come from the practice during colonial times of hiding illicit liquor in a flask tucked into the top of a boot. It became a common term during prohibition to describe alcohol suppliers. "Bootleg" today can mean pirated software, music, or even fashion brands.

booze An alcoholic beverage. Until the 1840s, the word was used as a verb and meant to drink a lot. Benjamin Franklin had noted that "boozy" was another word for drunk. During the election of 1840, one story goes, a distiller named Edmund

G. Booz of Philadelphia began selling Old Cabin Whiskey in bottles shaped like log cabins, in recognition of candidate William Henry Harrison, a "hard cider and log cabin man." Harrison won and the word became more commonly used, this time as a noun.

dry   An area where alcoholic beverages aren't served, or a person opposed to drinking booze. In the 1920s, it came in degrees: dryish, cracker dry, bone-dry, and most arid.

flapper   A young woman in the 1920s who lived somewhat recklessly, shunning corsets, cutting her hair short, wearing straight dresses with shorter hem lengths, and using makeup. The term probably came from a description of girls as young birds just on the verge of leaving the nest.

hooch   Slang for alcohol. Other slang words in the 1920s included "apple-jack," "giggle water," "white lightening," and "whoopee."

moonshine   Illegally manufactured liquor, often homemade. The term dates back as early as 1796 to refer to liquor smuggled under the cover of darkness to avoid government taxes.

ombibulous   A term coined by the newspaper writer H. L. Mencken to describe his support of all kinds of alcohol, despite prohibition. "I'm ombibulous. I drink every known alcoholic drink and enjoy them all," he said.

prohibition   The social movement to ban drinking, as well as the time between 1920 and 1933 when the Eighteenth Amendment banned the manufacture and sale of alcoholic beverages. It could have been the abstinence movement or something else. But the same activists involved in "abolition," or the fight to end slavery, were advocates of prohibition and may have chosen this rallying cry because it had a similar ring to "abolition."

real McCoy   An expression meaning "the real thing." First used in Scotland, where a drop of the "real MacKay," meant the real whiskey. In the United States, MacKay became McCoy, maybe referring to a boxer named Kid McCoy. Some also say it may have come from a rumrunner named William "Bill" McCoy, who was noted for delivering liquor that wasn't watered down.

rumrunner   A smuggler of illegal liquor, usually someone who brought liquor in from outside U.S. borders or over water.

speakeasy   An illegal drinking spot, often a nice bar that required an invitation or a secret password for entrance. Believed to come from bartenders' requests that patrons should be quiet and "speak easy" in it so they didn't draw attention to it.

teetotaler   A person who doesn't drink any alcoholic beverages. Believed to have come from early temperance societies. When people signed temperance pledges, some added a "T" to their names to indicate their "total" abstinence from all liquor. Putting the two together created "T-total."

temperance   Moderation or self-restraint in drinking alcoholic beverages. Derives from the Latin word for moderation or self-control.

Volsteadism   A common term for prohibition during the 1920s, referring to the Volstead Act, which defined what was and wasn't allowed under the Eighteenth Amendment. "Pre-Volstead" and "Post-Volstead" also were common, as was "Volsteadian."

wet   An area where alcoholic beverages are sold, or a person who supports legal drinking. In the 1920s, it came in degrees: dampish, moist, wettish, soaking wet, dripping, and wet as the Atlantic Ocean.

BIBLIOGRAPHY AND SOURCE NOTES

The most challenging part of researching the prohibition era and the years leading up to it was coming to terms with the mountains of material on the subject. In my first visit to a university library to start my work, I was completely overwhelmed. There weren't just several shelves of books and pamphlets—there were several *aisles*. Amid the histories were rows and rows of sermons and debates, different kinds of research arguing for and against the effects of alcohol, and publications from many states and cities, all wrestling with the "drink question" over a period of many years.

Those were just the temperance and prohibition sections. There were additional shelves on the Woman's Christian Temperance Union, the Anti-Saloon League, the repeal groups, and, of course, Al Capone and the other gangsters of the 1920s. And this library was just one resource. What quickly became clear was how enormous and divisive this issue had been for decades. From the late 1800s until the 1930s, the temperance movement and prohibition reached into virtually every corner and crevice of American life.

As a result, if you want to know more about it, you can start almost in your own neighborhood. Nearly all local, county, and state historical societies have photographs, news articles, and other original materials on prohibition, and libraries with a local history section will probably have a collection, too.

For a real taste of what the debates about prohibition were like, there's nothing like newspapers and magazine articles of the time. The *New York Times* is available and searchable online back to its beginnings, as is *Time* magazine. For relatively small fees, I was also able to search the archives of the *Boston Globe, Chicago Tribune, Los Angeles Times,* and *Washington Post,* and the entire *Dallas Morning News* archive was available online for free through the Dallas Public Library. The *New Yorker* archive is available to subscribers, and a few other magazines were available electronically through databases at university libraries.

I also read many other magazines, newspapers, and documents at the Dallas Public Library; the Southern Methodist University library (which has a rich collection of Anti-Saloon League yearbooks); the Library of Congress, in Washington, D.C.; the Morris Sheppard papers at the Center for American History at the University of Texas at Austin; Chicago History Museum Research Center; Rutger's Center of Alcohol Studies Library; the Woman's Christian Temperance Union library in Evanston, Illinois; and the Duke University library.

To find out more about what the prohibition years were like to a child, I sent interview requests to a half dozen famous people born just before 1920. Most who responded said that they didn't remember the time or weren't affected by it. But then-Supreme Court Justice John Paul Stevens called out of the blue one summer morning and shared his recollections about growing up in Chicago.

A few professors and authors also were incredibly gracious in sharing their wisdom and insights. My former *Wall Street Journal* colleague Jonathan Eig generously provided an early draft and an unpublished version of his new book on Al Capone, *Get Capone,* as well as a key newspaper article, and author Neal Thompson shared his knowledge about Raymond Parks. Catherine Gilbert Murdock, a Ph.D. and expert on women and prohibition, as well as a fabulous young-adult novelist, also took time to help guide me. James S. Roberts, an executive vice provost at Duke University and an expert on the social history of alcohol, kindly offered his thoughts and a reading list. Jonathan Zimmerman, a professor at New York University; K. Austin Kerr, a retired professor at Ohio State

University; and David Kyvig, professor at Northern Illinois University, also took my calls.

Here are the books I used.

RESOURCES ON PROHIBITION, TEMPERANCE, AND ALCOHOL

Allen, Frederick Lewis. *Only Yesterday: An Informal History of the 1920s.* New York: Harper & Row, Publishers, 1931.

Asbury, Herbert. *The Great Illusion: An Informal History of Prohibition.* Garden City, NY: Doubleday & Company, Inc., 1950.

Blocker, Jack S., Jr. *American Temperance Movements: Cycles of Reform.* Boston: Twayne Publishers, 1989.

————. *Retreat from Reform: The Prohibition Movement in the United States 1890–1913.* Westport, CT: Greenwood Press, 1976.

Burnham, J. C. "New Perspectives on the Prohibition 'Experiment' of the 1920's," *Journal of Social History* 2, no. 1 (Fall 1968): 51–68.

Burns, Eric. *The Spirits of America: A Social History of Alcohol.* Philadelphia: Temple University Press, 2004.

Carse, Robert. *Rum Row.* London: Jarrolds Publishers (London) Ltd., 1961.

Clark, Norman H. *Deliver Us from Evil: An Interpretation of American Prohibition.* New York and London: W. W. Norton & Company, 1976.

Coffey, Thomas M. *The Long Thirst: Prohibition in America: 1920–1933.* New York: W. W. Norton & Company Inc., 1975.

Einstein, Izzy. *Prohibition Agent No. 1.* New York: Frederick A. Stokes Company, 1932.

Engelmann, Larry. *Intemperance: The Lost War Against Liquor.* New York: The Free Press, 1979.

Everest, Allan S. *Rum Across the Border: The Prohibition Era in Northern New York.* Syracuse, NY: Syracuse University Press, 1978.

Furnas, J. C. *The Life and Times of the Late Demon Rum.* New York: Capricorn Books, 1973.

Kellner, Esther. *Moonshine: Its History and Folklore.* Indianapolis: The Bobbs-Merrill Company, 1971.

Kobler, John. *Ardent Spirits: The Rise and Fall of Prohibition*. New York: Da Capo Press, 1993.

Kyvig, David E. *Repealing National Prohibition*. Chicago: The University of Chicago Press, 1979.

Lender, Mark Edward, and James Kirby Martin. *Drinking in America: A History*. New York: The Free Press, 1982.

Lerner, Michael A. *Dry Manhattan: Prohibition in New York City*. Cambridge, MA: Harvard University Press, 2007.

Merz, Charles. *The Dry Decade*. Seattle: The University of Washington Press, 1930.

Okrent, Daniel. *Last Call: The Rise and Fall of Prohibition*. NY: Scribner, 2010.

Pegram, Thomas R. *Battling Demon Rum: The Struggle for a Dry America, 1800–1933*. Chicago: Ivan R. Dee, 1998.

Sinclair, Andrew. *Era of Excess: A Social History of the Prohibition Movement*. New York: Harper & Row, Publishers, 1962.

U.S. Wickersham Commission, *Enforcement of the Prohibition Laws, Official Records of the National Commission on Law Observance and Enforcement, Vol. 5*. Washington, D.C.: United States Government Printing Office, 1931.

Willebrandt, Mabel Walker. *The Inside of Prohibition*. Indianapolis: The Bobbs-Merrill Company, 1929.

Willoughby, Malcolm F. *Rum War at Sea*. Washington, D.C.: United States Government Printing Office, 1964.

RESOURCES ON MORRIS SHEPPARD

Bailey, Richard Ray. "Morris Sheppard of Texas: Southern Progressive and Prohibitionist." Ph.D. dissertation, Texas Christian University, August 1980.

Duke, Escal Franklin. "The Political Career of Morris Sheppard, 1875–1941." Ph.D. dissertation, University of Texas at Austin, May 1958.

Gould, Lewis. *Progressives and Prohibitionists: Texas Democrats in the Wilson Era*. Austin: University of Texas Press, 1973.

Keyes, Lucile Sheppard. "Morris Sheppard." Unpublished manuscript. Washington, D.C., with different page numbers in the versions at the SMU Library and the Center for American History at the University of Texas at Austin.

Salas, Karen Jeanette. "Senator Morris Sheppard and the Eighteenth Amendment," Master's thesis, University of Texas at Austin, August 1970.

Sheppard (Morris) Papers, 1894–1953, Dolph Briscoe Center for American History, The University of Texas at Austin.

BOOKS ON WOMEN AND THE WCTU

Bordin, Ruth. *Women and Temperance: The Quest for Power and Liberty, 1873–1900.* Philadelphia: Temple University Press, 1981.

Murdock, Catherine Gilbert. *Domesticating Drink: Women, Men, and Alcohol in America, 1870–1940.* Baltimore: The Johns Hopkins University Press, 1998.

Root, Grace. *Women and Repeal: The Story of the Women's Organization for National Prohibition Reform.* New York and London: Harper & Brothers Publishers, 1934.

Thompson, Eliza Jane Trimble, her two daughters, and Frances E. Willard. *Hillsboro Crusade Sketches and Family Records.* Cincinnati: Jennings and Graham, 1906.

Willard, Frances E. *Woman and Temperance, or the Work and Workers of the Woman's Christian Temperance Union.* New York: Arno Press, 1972.

Zimmerman, Jonathan. *Distilling Democracy: Alcohol Education in America's Public Schools, 1880–1925.* Lawrence, KS: University Press of Kansas, 1999.

BOOKS ON CARRIE NATION

Asbury, Herbert. *Carry Nation.* New York: Alfred A. Knopf, 1929.

Grace, Fran. *Carry A. Nation: Retelling the Life.* Bloomington: Indiana University Press, 2001.

Nation, Carry A. *The Use and Need of the Life of Carry A. Nation.* Topeka: F. M. Steves & Sons, 1905.

BOOKS ON THE ANTI-SALOON LEAGUE

Cherrington, Ernest H., ed. *The Anti-Saloon League Yearbook,* 1916 and 1919. Westerville, OH: American Issue Press.

Cherrington, Ernest H. *The Evolution of Prohibition in the United States of America: A Chronological History.* Westerville, OH: American Issue Press, 1920.

Kerr, K. Austin. *Organized for Prohibition: A New History of the Anti-Saloon League.* New Haven, CT: Yale University Press, 1985.

Nicholson, S.E., secretary. *Proceedings of the Fifteenth National Convention of the Anti-Saloon League of America Twenty Year Jubilee Convention.* Westerville, OH: American Issue, Nov. 10-13, 1913.

Odegard, Peter H. *Pressure Politics: The Story of the Anti-Saloon League.* New York: Columbia University Press, 1928.

BOOKS ON CARS AND HENRY FORD

Ford, Henry. *My Philosophy of Industry.* New York: Coward-McCann, Inc., 1929.

Menzer, Joe. *The Wildest Ride: A History of NASCAR.* New York: Simon & Schuster, 2002.

Sward, Keith. *The Legend of Henry Ford.* New York: Russell & Russell, 1968.

Thompson, Neal. *Driving with the Devil: Southern Moonshine, Detroit Wheels, and the Birth of NASCAR.* New York: Three Rivers Press, 2006.

Watts, Steven. *The People's Tycoon: Henry Ford and the American Century.* New York: Alfred A. Knopf, 2005.

BOOKS ON AL CAPONE

Eig, Jonathan. *Get Capone: The Secret Plot That Captured America's Most Wanted Gangster.* New York: Simon & Schuster, 2010.

Irey, Elmer L., as told to William J. Slocum. *The Tax Dodgers: The Inside Story of the T-Men's War with America's Political and Underworld Hoodlums.* Garden City, NY: Garden City Publishing Co., 1948.

Kobler, John. *Capone: The Life and World of Al Capone.* Cambridge, MA: Da Capo Press, 2003.

Nelli, Humbert S. *The Business of Crime: Italians and Syndicate Crime in the United States.* New York: Oxford University Press, 1976.

Pasley, Fred D. *Al Capone: The Biography of a Self-Made Man.* Salem, NH: Ayer Company, Publishers, 1930, reprinted 1971.

Schoenberg, Robert J. *Mr. Capone: The Real—and Complete—Story of Al Capone.* New York: William Morrow, 1992.

OTHER SOURCES

Basler, Roy P., ed. *Abraham Lincoln: His Speeches and Writings.* Cleveland and New York: The World Publishing Company, 1946.

Fass, Paula S. *The Damned and the Beautiful: American Youth in the 1920s.* Oxford: Oxford University Press, 1977.

Harper, Ida Husted. *Life and Work of Susan B. Anthony.* North Stratford, NH: Ayer Company Publishing Inc., reprint edition, 1998.

Hoover, Herbert. *The Memoirs of Herbert Hoover: The Cabinet and the Presidency, 1920–1933.* New York: The Macmillan Company, 1951. Accessed online at www.ecommcode.com/hoover/ebooks/browse.cfm.

Hu, Tun Yuan. *The Liquor Tax in the United States, 1791–1947.* New York: Columbia University Graduate School of Business, 1950.

Kyvig, David E. *Daily Life in America 1920–1940: How Americans Lived Through the Roaring Twenties and the Great Depression.* Chicago: Ivan R. Dee, 2004.

Longworth, Alice Roosevelt. *Crowded Hours: Reminiscences.* New York: Charles Scribner's Sons, 1933.

Ostransky, Leroy. *Sharkey's Kid: A Memoir.* New York: William Morrow and Company, Inc., 1991.

Ware, Caroline F. *Greenwich Village 1920–1930: A Comment on American Civilization in the Post-War Years.* Boston: Houghton-Mifflin, 1935.

FOR ADDITIONAL READING ON THE TIMES

Anti-Saloon League Web site: http://www.wpl.lib.oh.us/AntiSaloon/.

Bausum, Ann. *Unraveling Freedom: The Battle for Democracy on the Home Front During World War I.* Washington, D.C.: National Geographic, 2010.

Blumenthal, Karen. *Six Days in October: The Stock Market Crash of 1929.* New York: Atheneum, 2002.

Fitzgerald, F. Scott. *The Great Gatsby*. New York: Scribner, 1925. (A classic.)

Hill, Laban Carrick. *Harlem Stomp! A Cultural History of the Harlem Renaissance*. New York: Little, Brown and Company, 2003.

London, Jack. *John Barleycorn*. New York: The Modern Library, 2001. (The author's story of his battle with alcohol.)

Ness, Eliot, with Oscar Fraley. *The Untouchables*. Mattituck, NY: American Reprint Co., 1976. (Researchers say this account of trying to catch Al Capone is highly embellished, but it's an entertaining story that was made into movies and a television series.)

Sinclair, Upton. *The Flivver King*. Portway, England: Cedric Chivers Ltd., 1971. (A fictionalized account of Henry Ford and the Model T.)

————. *The Cup of Fury*. Great Neck, NY: Channel Press Inc., 1956.

SOURCE NOTES BY CHAPTER

(Topics are in the order in which they appear in the chapter.)

Valentine's Day 1929—Kobler, *Capone*, pp. 240–246. Schoenberg, *Mr. Capone*, pp. 207–215. Eig, *Get Capone*, pp.187–191.

Chapter 1: The Little Sheppard—Keyes, "Morris Sheppard," University of Texas version, pp. 21–25, 41. James B. Morrow, "Senator Was a 4-Year-Old Orator," *Boston Sunday Globe*, Dec. 26, 1915, from Sheppard (Morris) Papers, scrapbook 15, pp. 74–75. Thomas Carens, "The Man Behind Prohibition," *Arkansas Gazette Magazine*, from Sheppard (Morris) Papers, scrapbook 26, pp. 95–96. "Back to Texarkana," *Time*, Apr. 21, 1941, p. 26. Keyes, pp. 59–63. ***In Congress:*** "Youth Won in Texas," *Washington Post*, Dec. 14, 1902. "Talks With and About Members," *Washington Post*, Dec. 3, 1902. Keyes, pp. 83, 91. Duke, "The Political Career," pp. 127–154. ***1913 speech:*** "Sheppard in Speech Outlines His Course," *Dallas Morning News*, Jan. 30, 1913. "A Great Speech," *Kerrville Advance*, Sheppard (Morris) Papers, scrapbook 13, p. 116. ***Constitutional amendment:***

Asbury, *Great Illusion*, p. 126. "Rum Foes at Capitol," *Washington Post*, Dec. 11, 1913, p. 2. "Countrywide Prohibition Amendment Is Introduced," *Christian Science Monitor*, Dec. 11, 1913, p. 7. Congressional Record, 63rd Congress, 2nd session, Dec. 10, 1913, pp. 615–616.

Chapter 2: Hot and Cold Water—Lender and Martin, *Drinking in America*, pp. 2–10. Asbury, *Great Illusion*, pp. 5–7. *George Washington:* Pegram, *Battling Demon Rum*, 1998, p. ix. Kobler, *Ardent Spirits*, pp. 32–33. John H. Fund, "Moonshine Patriot," *Wall Street Journal*, Feb. 21, 2007. Lender and Martin, pp. 31–32, 14. *Rush:* Benjamin Rush, M.D., "An Enquiry into the Effects of Spirituous Liquors upon the Human Body, and Their Influence upon the Happiness of Society" (printed by Thomas Bradford, in Front Street, four doors down from the Coffee House). Brian S. Katcher, "Benjamin Rush's Educational Campaign Against Hard Drinking," *American Journal of Public Health*, Feb. 1993, p. 273, www.ajph.org. Lender and Martin, pp. 37–39. Asbury, p. 28. *Whiskey Insurrection:* Hu, *Liquor Tax*, pp. 13–28. Kobler, *Ardent Spirits*, p. 25. *1800–1830:* Lender and Martin, pp. 40, 46–47. Asbury, pp. 4–13. Blocker, *American Temperance Movements*, pp. 9–10. Basler, *Abraham Lincoln*, pp. 134–135. Harper, *Life and Work of Susan B. Anthony,* pp. 17–18. Emory Holloway, editor's introduction to Walter Whitman, *Franklin Evans or the Inebriate: A Tale of the Times*, NY: Random House, 1929, pp. v–xi. Furnas, *The Life and Times*, pp. 126–127. William M. Clark, "Ten Nights in a Bar Room," *American Heritage* magazine, June 1964, www.AmericanHeritage.com. *Cold Water Armies:* Asbury, pp. 51–52. Excerpt from Mary Livermore's autobiography, *The Story of My Life*, from the Old Sturbridge Village Online Resource Library, www.osv.org. Kobler, pp. 69–70. *1840s–1850s:* Lender and Martin, p. 196. Asbury, pp. 56–62.

Chapter 3: Home Destroyers and Defenders—Asbury, *Great Illusion*, pp. 70–71, 62–63. Willard, *Woman and Temperance*, pp. 54–57. Dio Lewis's full name was spelled as Diocletian and Dioclesian in various sources. Kobler, *Ardent Spirits*, pp. 172–176. Sinclair, *Era of Excess*, pp. 73–76. Perry R. Duis, "Saloons," *Encyclopedia of Chicago*, www.encyclopedia .chicagohistory.org. *Women drank, too:* Murdock, *Domesticating Drink*, pp. 49–63. *Hillsboro:* Thompson, *Hillsboro Crusade Sketches*, p. 73. Burns, *Spirits of America*, pp. 99–108. Kobler, pp. 114–126. Lender and Martin, *Drinking in America*, pp. 96–99. Asbury, pp. 79,

80–85. **WCTU:** "WCTU Drinking Fountains," compiled by Sarah F. Ward, National Woman's Christian Temperance Union booklet, 2007, pp. 1, 76–77. Kobler, pp. 131–146. Asbury, pp. 86–87. Willard, pp. 31–32. WCTU newsletters and materials from the WCTU. Murdock, p. 57. **Scientific Temperance:** Willard, pp. 251–254. Norton Mezvinsky, "Scientific Temperance Instruction in the Schools," *History of Education Quarterly* 1, no. 1 (Mar. 1961): 48–54. Zimmerman, *Distilling Democracy*, pp. 21, 93, 87. *Child's Health Primer for Primary Classes*, New York: A. S. Barnes and Company, 1885, pp. 25, 33, 41, 43, 53. Charles H. Stowell M.D., *A Primer of Health for Primary Classes*, New York: Silver, Burdett & Company, 1892, p. 73. *Physiology for Young People, Adapted to Intermediate Classes and Common Schools*, New York: American Book Company, 1888. Joel Dorman Steele, Ph.D., *Hygenic Physiology*, New York: American Book Company, 1888. Owen P. White, "Lips that Touch Liquor—," *Collier's*, Mar. 6, 1926, pp. 9–10, 38.

Chapter 4: A Nation Divides—Grace, *Carry A. Nation*, pp. 42–49, 100–101, 131–133, 139–144, 152–154, 180. Asbury, *Carry Nation*, pp. 25–32, 61, 63–67, 82–84, 100–104, 107–116, 164. Nation, *Use and Need of the Life*, pp. 36–37, 56, 71–72, 76–78. From www.nytimes.com: "Smashes Mirrors in Saloons," *New York Times*, Dec. 28, 1900; "Mrs. Nation Begins Her Crusade Anew," Jan. 22, 1901; "Mrs. Nation at Work Again," Jan. 24, 1901; "Mrs. Nation Horsewhipped," Jan. 25, 1901; "Mob Threatens Mrs. Nation," Jan. 27, 1901; "One More for Mrs. Nation," Feb. 6, 1901; "Mrs. Nation Returns to 'Joint' Smashing," Feb. 18, 1901; "Carrie Nation Dead," June 10, 1911.

Chapter 5: War!—Odegard, *Pressure Politics*, p. 4. Rev. Howard H. Russell, "Our League, God's Plan," in the *Proceedings, Fifteenth National Convention of the Anti-Saloon League of America Twenty Year Jubilee Convention*, Nov. 10–13, 1913, pp. 89–90, 93. Cherrington, *Evolution of Prohibition*, p. 253. **Saloons:** "Miss Addams on the Saloon," *Chicago Daily Tribune*, Mar. 31, 1902, p. 12. Arthur Huntington Gleason, "The Saloon in New York," *Collier's*, May 2, 1908, pp. 12–13, 27–28. Meridel LeSuer, "Beer Town," *Life in the United States*, New York: Charles Scribner's Sons, 1933, pp. 31–41. "The Experience and Observations of a New York Saloon-Keeper," *McClure's Magazine*, Jan. 1909, pp. 302–312. The term "rushing the growler" baffled many word experts. This explanation comes from various beer Web sites. For a different perspective, see "Word for the Wise," Jan. 16, 2009, www.merriam-webster.com and www.worldwidewords.org. **Saloon corruption:** Odegard, pp. 41–46. Kobler, *Ardent Spirits*, p. 177. Sinclair, *Era of Excess*, pp. 76–77. **Anti-Saloon League Progress:** Cherrington, p. 255. "March of Prohibition," *Washington Post*, Dec. 29, 1907, p. 3. Odegard, pp. 139–145. Asbury, pp. 124–125. **National law:** Wayne B. Wheeler, "The Inside Story of Prohibition's Adoption, Article I: Laying the Foundation for National Prohibition," *New York Times*, Mar. 28, 1926. "A Prohibition Nation in 1920—Why?" *The Union Signal*, Dec. 18, 1913, p. 5. "Crusade for Prohibition: Would Make This a Saloonless Nation," *Los Angeles Times*, Nov. 30, 1913, p. V16. Norborne Robinson, "Leaders Fearful of Prohibition," *Boston Daily Globe*, Dec. 10, 1913, p. 1. **"Open fire":** Wayne B. Wheeler, "The Inside Story of Prohibition's Adoption, Article II: Organizing for National Prohibition," *New York Times*, Mar. 29, 1926. Odegard, pp. 47–67, 73–77, 251–262. Murdock, *Domesticating Drink*, pp. 28–30, 82–87. Clark, *Deliver Us from Evil*, pp. 116–117. **War:** Sinclair, pp. 120–129. Odegard, pp. 67–72. Wayne B. Wheeler, "The Inside Story of Prohibition's Adoption, Article III: Lining Up Congress for Prohibition," *New York Times*, Mar. 30, 1926. **Wilson/Hughes:** www.woodrowwilson.org. Clark, pp. 127–128. "President Refuses to Concede Defeat," *New York Times*, Nov. 8, 1916. **Constitutional amendment:** William G. Shepherd, "Who Laughs Last," *Collier's*, Sept. 21, 1929. Congressional Record, 71st Congress, 1st Session, Sept. 14, 1929, pp. 3611–3614. Mark L. Goodwin, "Sheppard Raps Collier's Story on Prohibition," *Dallas Morning News*, Sept. 15, 1929. Merz, *Dry Decade*, pp. 28–36. Asbury, pp. 129–137. "House Passes Dry Amendment," *Boston Daily Globe*, Dec. 18, 1917, p. 1. "Prohibition Wins in National House by 282 to 128," *New York Times*, Dec. 18, 1917. "House, 176–55, Overrides Veto of War Prohibition," *New York Times*, Oct. 28, 1919. "House Passes Prohibition Bill Over President Wilson's Veto," *Dallas Morning News*, Oct. 28, 1919.

Chapter 6: Dry!—Asbury, *Great Illusion*, pp. 142, 144–46. "John Barleycorn Takes Final Count in Nation," *Boston Daily Globe*, Jan. 17, 1920, p. 1. "John Barleycorn Died Peacefully at the Toll of 12," *New York Times*, Jan. 17, 1920, p. 1. John Larson, "Growing Up in St. Paul," *Ramsey County History* 35, no. 4 (Winter 2001): 24. "Bryan at Capital 'Wake,'" and "Billy Sunday Speeds Barleycorn to Grave," both in *New York Times*, Jan.

17, 1920. **Librarians:** "Midnight Ends Reign of Booze," *Los Angeles Times*, Jan. 16, 1920. "Federal Stage Set for Dry Law Entry Tomorrow," *New York Times*, Jan. 16, 1920. "John Barleycorn's 'Wake' Very Wet," *Boston Daily Globe*, Jan. 16, 1920, p. 1. **Other impact:** www.anheuser-busch.com/history.html. Jeremiah McWilliams, "75 Years After the End of Prohibition," *St. Louis Post-Dispatch,* Apr. 6, 2008. Merz, p. 329. Lerner, *Dry Manhattan*, pp. 50–51. Kyvig, *Daily Life*, p. 113. "Demon Rum Is Counted Out," *Los Angeles Times*, Jan. 16, 1920, Section III, p. 3. Kobler, *Ardent Spirits*, pp. 250–251. "Drought Costs Rabbi His Job," *Los Angeles Times*, Mar. 13, 1921, p. 115. **Sheppard's still:** "Still on Senator's Farm," *New York Times*, Sept. 7, 1920. Bailey, "Morris Sheppard of Texas," p. 92. **Rumrunners:** Carse, *Rum Row*, pp. 15–57. Asbury, pp. 247–250. Wayne Curtis, "Bootleg Paradise," *American Heritage*, Apr./May 2007, pp. 70–76. Michael Quinion, www.Worldwidewords.org. "Speakeasy," *American Speech* 59, no. 3 (Autumn 1984): 268–269. **Leroy Ostransky:** Ostransky, *Sharkey's Kid*, pp. 27–28, 89–103. "Wet Words in Kansas," *American Speech* 4, no. 5 (June 1929): 387. Ware, *Greenwich Village*, p. 54. Lerner, pp. 215–218. Kyvig, pp. 22–23. **Izzy and Moe:** Herbert Asbury, "When Prohibition Was in Flower," *American Mercury* 63 (July 1947): 41. Einstein, *Prohibition Agent No. 1.* John K. Winkler, "Izzy and Moe Stop the Show," *Collier's*, Feb. 6, 1926, pp. 15, 38. "Sees Izzy and Moe, Bartender Faints," *New York Times*, July 17, 1922. Truman H. Talley, "Einstein, Rum Sleuth," *New York Times*, Mar. 26, 1922.

Chapter 7: Milk and Moonshine—Sinclair, *Era of Excess*, pp. 278–279. "Washington's Prohibition Farce," *New York Times*, Jan. 14, 1923. Edward T. Folliard, "White House Hedge Hid Bootleg Gin," *Washington Post*, Dec. 6, 1953, p. B1. Longworth, *Crowded Hours*, pp. 313–316, 324. E-mail with Jean Craighead George, June 26, 2008. Phone interview with Justice John Paul Stevens, June 30, 2008. Kyvig, *Daily Life*, p. 24. **Politics:** Cora Frances Stoddard and Amy Woods, "Fifteen Years of the Drink Question in Massachusetts," reprints from Winter 1928 and Spring 1929 *Scientific Temperance Journals*, Westerville, OH: American Issue Publishing Company, 1930. Sinclair, p. 248. "Find Sober Men Critical," *New York Times*, Apr. 13, 1922. Keyes, "Morris Sheppard," p. 200. Asbury, *Great Illusion*, p. 317. Merz, *Dry Decade*, pp. 218–219. **Prohibition and the**

young: Fass, *The Damned and the Beautiful,* pp. 310–321. James A. Maxwell, "To the Malt Add Hops," *Chicago, vol.* 2, no. 1 (Apr. 1954): 26–29. Everest, *Rum Across the Border,* pp. 19–23. **Detroit:** James C. Young, "In the 'Rum Capital' of Dry America," *New York Times,* July 14, 1929. Engelmann, *Intemperance,* pp. 107, 99–100. Asbury, p. 160. "Boy, 14, Slave to Moonshine," *Detroit News,* Mar. 8, 1924, p. 1. "A Child Rebels: Tells Police How Blind Pigs Have School Victims," *Detroit News,* Mar. 9, 1924, p. 1. "The Parlor Pig Law's Bugaboo," *Detroit News,* Mar. 23, 1924, p. 1. **Drinks:** "Washington's Prohibition Farce," *New York Times,* Jan. 14, 1923. William G. Shepherd, "Kansas, by Ginger!" *Collier's,* July 26, 1929, pp. 12–13, 48, 50. Kobler, *Ardent Spirits,* pp. 301–309, 239–240. Sinclair, pp. 209, 205. Asbury, pp. 280, 277. Owen P. White, "Dripping Dry Dallas," *Collier's,* July 20, 1929, p. 8. Kellner, *Moonshine,* pp. 112–113. Albert W. Fox, "Nation-Wide Rise in Drinking Under Dry Law Reported," *Washington Post,* Apr. 14, 1926. **Ford:** Sinclair, pp. 316–318. Sward, *Legend of Henry Ford,* pp. 58–61. "The Model T Put the World on Wheels," Ford Motor Co., http://www.ford.com/about-ford/heritage/vehicles/modelt/672-model-t. Samuel Crowther, "Prohibition or Poverty: An Interview with Henry Ford," *Ladies Home Journal,* Apr. 1930, pp. 35, 225. "Ford Urges Army Keep Country 'Dry,'" *New York Times,* June 10, 1923. **Parks:** Eddie Samples, "GaRHoFa's Raymond Dawson Parks," Georgia Automobile Racing Hall of Fame Association newsletter, *Pioneer Pages* 5, no. 1 (Feb. 2002). Thompson, *Driving with the Devil,* pp. 15–43. Kellner, pp. 56–60. Sinclair, p. 319.

Chapter 8: Snorky and Scarface—Patricia Dougherty, "Gang Boundaries, Not Wards, Divide Chicago, Says 'Scarface Al,'" *Chicago Herald-Examiner,* Mar. 9, 1927, article provided by Jonathan Eig. Eig, *Get Capone,* p. 103. "'You Can All Go Thirsty' Is Al Capone's Adieu," *Chicago Daily Tribune,* Dec. 6, 1927. **Born in 1899:** Kobler, *Capone,* pp. 18, 27, 31, 35–37, 67, 101–103, 266. Schoenberg, *Mr. Capone,* pp. 21, 30–36, 179, 182. **"We figured this law . . .":** Patricia Dougherty, "Booze: A Woman Reporter's Inside Story of the Most Extraordinary Situation in the United States," *Hearst's International—Cosmopolitan,* Apr. 1927, pp. 34–35ff. "Capone Aid Arraigned; Bail Denied," Oct. 12, 1931, unidentified newspaper article, Capone Scrapbook, Chicago History Society. **Cicero to McSwiggin:** Kobler, pp. 114–115, 119–120, 128–129, 148 Schoenberg, pp. 96–99, 102–103, 182. F. Raymond Daniell, "The Big Business of the Racketeers," *New York Times*, Apr. 27, 1930. S. J. Duncan-Clark, "'Scarface' Al Capone Has Never Run Away," *New York Times,* May 26, 1929. "Coming Out Party," *Time*, Mar. 24, 1930. Patricia Dougherty, "Gang Boundaries" and "Booze." Kobler, p. 15. Eig, pp. 64, 103. ***Prohibition agents:*** "Full Text of the Wickersham Commission Report on Prohibition," *New York Times*, Jan. 21, 1931. ***Two-Gun:*** Kobler, pp. 375–376. *Two-Gun Hart and Al Capone: The Story of Two Italian Brothers*, Lincoln, NE: The "Two-Gun" Project and JC&H Productions, 2000. This book contains a series of news clippings detailing Hart's arrests and exploits, apparently compiled by family members. But Kobler paints a different picture, writing that Hart was twice charged with murder (though never convicted), and eventually lost his job as town marshall of Homer, NE., for stealing. "A 'White Sheep' Capone Found—A Police Officer!" *New York Times*, Sept. 20, 1951. "Ex-Judge, A Capone, Dies," *New York Times*, Dec. 2, 1952. ***St. Valentine's Massacre:*** Kobler, pp. 240–254. Schoenberg, pp. 207–229, 241–242. Eig, pp.187–194, 198–210, 247–253. "'Hoodlum," *Time*, Nov. 20, 1939. "Slay Doctor in Massacre," *Chicago Daily Tribune*, Feb. 15, 1929, p. 1.

Chapter 9: Wet, Again—Inaugural Address of Herbert Hoover, The Avalon Project at Yale Law School, Avalon.law.yale.edu/20th_century/hoover.asp. "Harding Pledges Dry Enforcement," *New York Times*, June 26, 1923. Kyvig, *Repealing National Prohibition*, p. 45. Merz, *Dry Decade*, p. 224. Clark, *Deliver Us*, pp. 183–197. Sinclair, *Era of Excess*, pp. 292–306. Hoover, *Memoirs*, p. 201. ***AAPA:*** Kyvig, pp. 2, 105–109. John C. Gebhart, "Movement Against Prohibition," *Annals of the American Academy of Political and Social Science* 163 (Sept. 1932): 172–180. "Scandals of Prohibition Enforcement," Mar. 1, 1929, and "Cost of Prohibition and Your Income Tax," May 1929, pamphlets published by the Association Against the Prohibition Amendment, Washington, D.C. ***Sabin:*** Pauline Morton Sabin, "I Change My Mind on Prohibition," *The Outlook*, June 13, 1928, pp. 254, 272. "Ladies at Roslyn," *Time*, July 18, 1932. Kyvig, p. 117, 122. Root, *Women and Repeal,* pp. xii–xiii. Asbury, *Great Illusion*, p. 315. ***Morris Sheppard:*** Harry Benge Crozier, "Convention Names Townsend Permanent Chairman," *Dallas Morning News*, Sept. 10, 1930. ***Problems with prohibition:*** Merz, pp. 330–331. "Full Prisons Check Dry

Enforcement," *New York Times,* Apr. 17, 1930. "Hoover Backs Mass Drive to Stamp Out Crime Rings," *New York Times*, Apr. 30, 1930. Blumenthal, *Six Days*, pp. 118, 132. **Capone:** Hoover, *Memoirs*, pp. 276–277. Schoenberg, *Mr. Capone,* pp. 241–250. Eig, *Get Capone*, pp. 220–367. Capone scrapbooks, Chicago History Museum. **Repeal:** H. I. Brock, "Our Speakeasies Consider Their Future," *New York Times*," Sept. 11, 1932. Sinclair, pp. 339, 365–375. "Drys Are Resentful, Wet Chiefs Jubilant," *New York Times,* June 8, 1932. W. A. Warn, "Result Cheered Wildly," *New York Times,* June 30, 1932. "Convention Throng Hails Roosevelt," *New York Times*, July 3, 1932. "Senator Sheppard," *Washington Post*, Apr. 10, 1941, p. 10. "21st Amendment," *Time,* Feb. 27, 1933. Kyvig, pp. 167–178. **Sheppard:** All from *Dallas Morning News*: Mark L. Goodwin, "Sheppard Coming Home to Campaign for Prohibition," July 28, 1933; "Sheppard Opens State Campaign Against Repeal," Aug. 2, 1933; "Sheppard Pleads for Dry Success," Aug. 3, 1933; "Repeal Sentiment Scored by Sheppard," Aug. 11, 1933; "Sheppard Didn't Lose," Sept. 17, 1933. Also, "Repeal Margin in Texas Gains on Late Count," *Washington Post,* Aug. 28, 1933, p. 3. "Humming Bird to Mars," *Time,* Sept. 4, 1933. **Final approval:** "Signing Ceremony Brief, Colorful," *New York Times,* Dec. 6, 1933. "Dry Era End Proclaimed on Utah's Ratification," *Los Angeles Times*, Dec. 6, 1933, p. 1. Cheers Mark Action by Utah," *Los Angeles Times*, Dec. 6, 1933, p. 6. "New Yorkers Celebrate John Barleycorn Return," *Los Angeles Times*, Dec. 6, 1933, p. 8. "Legalized Liquor Is Available to About Half the Population," *Chicago Daily Tribune*, Dec. 6, 1933, p. 2. "No Liquor Licenses to Be Issued in Dallas, But Druggists' Prices Defeating Bootleggers," *Dallas Morning News*, Dec. 6, 1933.

Epilogue: Success or Failure?—*Shoes:* Franklyn Waltman Jr., "The 58-Year-Old Dean of Congress," *Washington Post*, Apr. 22, 1934, p. SM3. "Bathtub Gin Era Began 20 Years Ago," *Washington Post*, Jan. 17, 1940, p. 16. "Senator Sheppard," *Washington Post,* Apr. 10, 1941, p. 10. Schoenberg, *Mr. Capone*, pp. 329–354. "A. J. Volstead Dies; Father of 'Dry' Act," *New York Times,* Jan. 21, 1947. Lender and Martin, *Drinking in America*, pp. 196–197. J. C. Burnham, "New Perspectives on the Prohibition 'Experiment' of the 1920s," *Journal of Social History* 2, no. 1 (Fall 1968): 59–61. R. L. Duffus, "Liquor Returns, But America Is Changed," *New York Times*, Dec. 3, 1933. Clark, *Deliver Us*, pp. 145–157. Temperance and

Prohibition Web site at Ohio State University, http://prohibition.osu.edu/brewing/consumption.cfm. Stevens interview, June 30, 2008. Lender and Martin, p. 181. National Institute on Alcohol Abuse and Alcoholism of the National Institutes of Health, www.niaaa.nih.gov. Mothers Against Drunk Driving, www.madd.org.; Enrique "Kiki" Camarena, http://www.justice.gov/dea/ongoing/red_ribbon/redribbon_history.html.

ACKNOWLEDGMENTS

Many years ago, when my youngest daughter was still new to kindergarten, she raced home with big, important news.

"Mommy, Mommy!" she exclaimed, her eyes shining with excitement. "Today I pledged to be drug-free!"

She was so enthusiastic, I had to congratulate her—and then wonder, as a parent, why a five-year-old needed to make such a pledge.

Years later, while reading about Susan B. Anthony's early life as an advocate for temperance and abstinence, long before she became a champion for a woman's right to vote, I flashed back to that moment. Here was a straight line from more than 150 years ago to today, one long, continuous worry about the impact of drugs and alcohol on our youngest citizens.

This story was born in that odd connection, a hope that maybe an understanding of this complex history would provide some important context to what has often been an emotional debate, perhaps leading to more discussion and a deeper meaning for the red ribbons that festoon my neighborhood every October.

In pulling together this story, I had a lot of help. I am especially grateful to Jonathan Eig, Austin Kerr, David Kyvig, Catherine Gilbert Murdock, Dan Okrent, Jim Roberts, Neal Thompson, Jonathan Zimmerman, and Jonathan Scott and Kelly Townsend of

Miles to Go Drug Education for helpful conversations. Janet Olson of the Frances Willard Memorial Library and Archives was especially generous in opening the doors there for me. The interlibrary loan professionals at the Dallas Public Library delivered, as always.

For assistance with photos, I am indebted to Jean Pierre Andrieux, who has a wonderful collection from St. Pierre & Miquelon; Jeff Bridgers of the Library of Congress Prints and Photographs Reading Room; Abby McCartney; Judit Ward at the Rutgers Center of Alcohol Studies Library; and Sonya Wind, daughter of Leroy Ostransky.

My agent Ken Wright embraced this idea from the very start, and there wouldn't be a book without him. Deirdre Langeland was the perfect editor, pushing and prodding in just the right ways; I hope this book is one she'll want to share with her own little one some years in the future. Deep appreciation goes to Jay Colvin for his patience and beautiful design, Jill Freshney for keeping us on track, and Andrea Cascardi for stepping in without skipping a single beat.

As always, I am thankful to my husband Scott McCartney, and my daughters, Abby and Jenny, who never wavered in their support, even in the face of yet another time-consuming obsession.

PICTURE CREDITS

Front cover: Hulton Archive/Getty Images; **Half title page:** fStop/Veer; **Title page:** Courtesy of Jean Pierre Andrieux; **Facing 1, 2:** Chicago History Museum; **4:** Bain Collection, Library of Congress; **7:** National Photo Company Collection, Library of Congress; **8, 9:** Sheppard (Morris) Papers, Dolph Briscoe Center for American History, University of Texas at Austin; **10:** Bettman/Corbis; **12:** Author's collection; **14:** Courtesy of the Mount Vernon Ladies' Association; **15:** Courtesy of the Rutgers University Center of Alcohol Studies Library; **16:** Currier & Ives, Library of Congress; **18, 19:** Hulton Archive, Getty Images; **22:** Ohio Historical Society; **24:** The Graphic, July 29, 1876, Library of Congress; **26:** Currier & Ives, Library of Congress; **28:** Courtesy of the Detroit Historical Society; **29:** Author's collection; **30:** From *Songs for Boys and Girls of the Loyal Temperance Legion*, (revised). (Evanston, IL: National WCTU Publishing House, undated.); **32:** Bain Collection, Library of Congress; **34:** AP Images; **36:** KansasMemory. org, Kansas State Historical Society; **37:** American Stock Archive/Getty Images; **38, 39, 40:** KansasMemory.org, Kansas State Historical Society; **42:** Photo by J.C. Lay, Library of Congress; **44:** Rushing the Growler, ca. 1890, Museum of the City of New York, Jacob. A. Riis Collection; **46:** Lewis W. Hine/Getty Images; **48, 49:** Library of Congress; **51:** Ohio Council on Alcohol Problems, Bentley Historical Library, University of Michigan; **53:** Author's collection; **55:** National Photo Company Collection, Library of

Congress; **56:** Harris & Ewing Collection, Library of Congress; **58:** Library of Congress; **61:** Library of Congress, Prints & Photographs Division, NYWT&S Collection; **62:** Brown Brothers; **64:** From *Rum Row* by Robert Carse, (Jarrolds Publishers (London) Ltd, 1961); **65:** Courtesy of Sonya Wind; **66:** Library of Congress; **68:** Underwood & Underwood/Getty Images; **70:** Underwood & Underwood/Corbis; **72:** New York Daily News Archives/Getty Images; **74:** Library of Congress, Prints & Photographs Division, NYWT&S Collection; **76:** Brown Brothers; **77:** From the Atlanta Constitution, Jan 26, 1923; **78:** National Photo Company Collection, Library of Congress; **79:** Brown Brothers; **81:** Detroit News, March 17, 1924, p. 1; **82:** Author's collection; **84:** Underwood & Underwood, Library of Congress; **85:** Library of Congress; **87:** Bettman/Corbis; **88:** Courtesy of the Georgia Automobile Racing Hall of Fame Association; **90:** APA/Getty Images; **93:** By permission of Rollin Kirby Post; **95:** Chicago History Museum; **96:** Library of Congress; **99:** Chicago History Museum; **100:** New York Times Co./Getty Images; **103:** State Historical Society of North Dakota 1952-0088; **104:** Chicago History Museum; **106:** Library of Congress, Prints & Photographs Division, NYWT&S Collection; **108:** National Photo Company Collection, Library of Congress; **110:** Underwood & Underwood, Library of Congress; **112:** Courtesy of the Hagley Museum & Library; **113:** AP Images; **114:** Library of Congress, Prints & Photographs Division, NYWT&S Collection; **117:** National Photo Company Collection, Library of Congress; **119:** Milstein Division of United States History, Local History & Genealogy, The New York Public Library, Astor, Lenox and Tilden Foundations; **120:** Library of Congress, Prints & Photographs Division, NYWT&S Collection; **122:** By permission of Rollin Kirby Post; **126:** Bettman/Corbis; **127:** AP Images; **Back cover:** Library of Congress, Prints and Photographs Division.

INDEX

Numbers in **bold** indicate pages with illustrations